23 secret Keys

Unlocking How-to Forever

Way Better Your L.I.F.E^2.

Tactics

(Book-three)

Create Pro-habits

that get you

What You TRULY Want

and stop letting

Chaos-habits Limit Your Possibilities

Produced by:

Living Perspectives Publishing

Feedback email: DavidHastingsTheAuthor@gmail.com

Dr. David J. Hastings PhD

23 secret *Keys*

Unlocking How-to Forever

Way Better Your L.I.F.E^2.

Tactics
(Book-three)

Create Pro-habits

that get you

What You TRULY Want

and stop letting

Chaos-habits Limit Your Possibilities

Overview

If interested in finding out about what makes you "**DO** what you **DO**" and how all that actually works, **so that you can take back control of YOU** and *Way Better* Your L.I.F.E^2., read on.

Every second of every day, a marvelous array of automated **Body-Self** and **Mind-Self** mechanisms drive countless outbound actions that have but a singular, primary mandate: keep us physically safe and surviving.

Incredibly, although **Body-Self** and **Mind-Self** (called the **Self-Duo**) outbound actions are designed and propelled by significantly different processes (detailed in Book-one and Book-two, respectively), one methodology is similar. Both frequency compare **current-new** to **archived-old**.

In other words, each Self-Duo system **Comparatively-Analyzes** inbound or current-new sensory-information (the fundamental source of all we know or will ever know), to previously stored or data-archived sensory-information or **fodder**, called archived-old to design not only outbound Body-Self habitual-actions but also Mind-Self **living-experiences**.

Problem is, especially when during formative years current-new is provided via abusive environments, archived-old are populated not with joyful contiguous experiences but instead with high-energy nightmarish fragments.

As archived-old is compromised, so too is Comparative-Analysis and Mind-Self Figure-It-Out processing negatively skewed. **Sensory-skewing** thus leaves self-doubt, addictions, destructive behaviours and low self-esteem in its wake.

Currently, the *Way Better* Your **L.I.F.E^2.** series is comprised of three books: *Body-Self*, *Mind-Self* and *Tactics*.

L.I.F.E^2. is this author abbreviation or acronym for
Living In Full Experience and Excitement.

Throughout the series are revealed **23 secret keys** that will **FOREVER** unlock how to *Way Better* Your L.I.F.E^2.: This is the series purpose.

Although free to read or listen to the books in any order, I suggest an additional strategy to sequential.

Overview

Begin with Book-three, *Way Better* Your L.I.F.E^2.: **Tactic**s. It contains great summaries of the first two books.

Then, as topics are mentioned in **Tactics**, use the first two books as resources to reference much deeper How-We-Work understandings and corresponding research driven proofs.

The Trilogy's mandate is accomplished in three stages: First, establish a consistent, irrefutable new-thought foundation for Book-three (*Tactics*) discussions by dissolving myths and misconceptions about the functional roles and interactions of *Body* and *Mind* (books one and two).

In other words, Book-one and Book-two fully explain for the first time the driving mechanisms, which demarcate **How-We-Truly-Work**. They clearly and systematically unlock both the inbound and outbound *Body-Self* and *Mind-Self* functionalities and interactions that are **Key** to understanding **How-We-Truly-Work**.

More comprehensively, the two initial books, *Way Better* Your L.I.F.E^2.: *Body-Self* and *Way Better* Your L.I.F.E^2.: *Mind-Self*, illuminate not only the many fascinating neurological and physiological facilities, mechanisms and activities of Body-Self and Mind-Self (coined the **Self-Duo**) but also among many other new and exciting revelations, the steadfast and extraordinary interactions between Body-Self and Mind-Self that make you, **YOU**.

> Together, they provide needed transparency to the many varied aspects of not only the simpler habitual primary-responses of Body-Self but also the significantly more intricate **Figure-It-Out** processing and habitual cognitive-behaviours of Mind-Self.

They thus provide an unassailable foundation for the comprehensive, yet clear and easy to grasp, **living-condition** enhancement discussions contained in book three, *Way Better* Your L.I.F.E^2.: *Tactics*.

> *Tactics* focuses on prime areas that have the greatest potential to *Way Better* Your L.I.F.E^2.: **Health** (physical and mental), **Relationships** (with yourself, significant person and others) and **Wealth** (both joyfulness and material).

Second, purposed to enable effective actions that enhance rather than diminish L.I.F.E^2., *Tactics*, among many other revelations builds upon the **How-We-Truly-**

Overview

Work principles presented in the first two books to expansively detail how to disengage detrimental **chaos-habits**: such as, addictions, disparaging self-talk, destructive and abusive behaviours toward 'self-and-others' and the like.

Stated differently, if one knew how **chaos-habits** form and how to disarm their detrimental agendas, one could bypass them and instead create new beneficial **Pro-habits** that automatically would fulfill (as this is their inherent design) all wishes and dreams.

One might state:
If it wasn't for my chaos-habits relentlessly limiting my options 24/7
and negatively skewing my perceptions …

I would already have everything I **TRULY** want!

Thirdly, *Tactics* instructs how to both create productive or P**ro-habits** that absolutely and effortlessly will get you what you **TRULY** want and how to make them the **GO-TO** instead of their currently hardened chaos-habit counterparts.

In other words, *Tactics* provides powerful methodologies that explain how to create productive or **pro-habits** that will strive automatically and relentlessly (as this is their nature) to get you what you **TRULY** want; while simultaneously disarming **chaos-habits** (like addictions, negative self-talk, compulsive and destructive behaviours, and the like) *that are keeping you from becoming all you can be*.

Understanding how to create and deploy these two Keys alone will leap anyone toward significantly maximizing both **L.I.F.E^2.** and positive **living-experiences**.

Additionally, *Tactics* delivers many other clear-cut **Keys** or deployment methodologies that will FOREVER unlock how to get what you **TRULY** want.

Expansively, the series also illuminates the foundational symmetry between our underlying **How-We-Work** functionality and the Laws of our **Universe-H**: coined as such in *Way Better* Your L.I.F.E^2.: *Body-Self*.

Overview

Deeper

One might justifiably ask, "Was it so important to understand **How-We-Truly-Work** that two books were needed"?

Let me suggest as undeniable that when one is unaware of how 'something' works and/or its purpose – be it the 'quick' check-in Kiosk at the airport, the cellphone application on your hand-held computer, the T.V. remote control or the Universe – speculations about its utility will be grossly deficient.

> In other words, when one is minimally knowledgeable about either how something works or its capabilities, one's alternative is random guessing.

Therefore, as haphazard assumptions result in mostly inaccurate and minimally useful conclusions, one should strive to improve decisions by fully understanding not only how 'things' but also especially **How-We-Work** based not on conjecture but on in depth irrefutable evidences.

> Conclusively, guessing **How-We-Work** as people is clearly no way to run one's life.

Without question then, one profound benefit derived by both learning **How-We-Truly-Work** and comprehending the *Way Better* Your L.I.F.E^2. series perspectives is that choices and decisions will no longer be based on 'random guessing' about one's functional drivers.

In other words, undeniable is that understanding **How-We-Truly-Work** (in lieu of guessing) is the vastly superior route to *Way Better* Your **L.I.F.E^2.**

> In short, the Trilogy first exposes what drives us and makes us **DO** what we **DO**, then offers *Tactics* that hugely enhance one's **living-experiences** - FOREVER.

Consistent with the above, I believe that a competent self-help series, prior to offering strategies for enhancing one's life and explaining **How-We-Work** habitually, physiologically, cognitively, psychologically, etc. should first thoroughly explain the responsible front-line bio-mechanical and physiological gateway mechanisms that facilitate experiencing a portion of the wonders, which Bombard us 24/7 from the vast **Out-There**.

Overview

In other words, to *Way Better* Your L.I.F.E^2., necessary is a reasonable understanding of how our physiology or living-systems (such as, sensory-receptors, brain-mass, neural mechanisms, hormonal drivers, etc.) work and interact to produce the action-outcomes that flow us through our days, weeks, months and years.

> Most do not realize that everything one 'knows', everything one 'understands' and everything one can 'become' originates with **sensory-acceptance**.

Consequently, the *Way Better* Your L.I.F.E^2. journey initiates with the events from the **Out-There**, which impact one's **sensory-arrays**.

Fantastically, one's various types of sensory-array equipment are designed to first selectively sensory-accept information (called **current-new** once accepted) from the **Out-There** and second, initialize a chain of neurological actions.

Neurological actions culminate with delivery of action-potential to various cerebral processor mechanisms that morph the action-potential into **neurological-currency** or **fodder**. Current-new fodder is utilized for **comparative-analysis** of current-new to frequency applicable **archived-old** (i.e., storehoused experiences) in order to keep us safe and maximize survival potential.

In other words, only by understanding the purposes behind why inbound action-potential is morphed and evaluated along its route from sensory-acceptance to ultimate storehousing as **fodder** in **data-archives**, can the full **How-We-Truly-Work** story be told.

> The brief reason for the myriads of *Body-Self* and *Mind-Self* evaluative processes is to avoid danger and seek Solution: i.e., keep us safe and improve surrounding **living-conditions**. These enormous feats are accomplished by employing multiple **comparative-analysis** neural-processors, which first recall and then compare current-new to frequency applicable archived-old.

Thus, among many other associated *Way Better* Your L.I.F.E^2. mandates, the series exposes not only **How-We-Truly-Work** but also how one becomes who one is, why one does what they DO, how to unlock one's genetically provisioned, previously inaccessible capabilities and capacities, and more expansively, how Humanity fits into and provide an essential component to the Universe.

Overview

Relentlessly, every millisecond of every day, all sensory-array event-horizons are being pummelled by potentially catastrophic events originating from the vast **Out-There**.

> Thus, the importance of sensory-apparatus cannot be overstated. Collectively they are one's only interface with the **Deluge**.

As such, **sensory-arrays** are exclusively responsible for not only providing the raw information about what is going-on **Out-There** but also defining, through physical movements, one's interactions and feedback collaborations with the unpredictable **Out-There**.

Incredibly, each specialized sensory-structure is responsible for first sensory-accepting only its particular frequency range (this is why the eyes don't hear and the ears don't see) and then morphing the 'impact' mechanical-energy into a unique action-potential '**signature**'.

Even more amazingly, when cerebral neural-processors further morph the action-potential into **fodder** and then storehouse it in multiple interactive data-archives, **fodder** becomes the **neurological-currency** of sentience.

> Thus, **fodder** accumulation in concert with its subsequent multi-purposed retrieval encompasses 100% of everything one now knows or will ever know!

Book-one propels the reader through fascinating enjoyable virtual voyages beginning from **Out-There** Bombardment on *Body-Self* sensory-arrays, then through all the fascinating and diverse neural and biological mechanisms that ultimately manifest one's vast assortment of perspectives and behavioral expressions and thus personality (Book-two): i.e., one's likes, dislikes, attractions, addictions and so much, much more.

While disclosing the many Body-Self and Mind-Self processes that relentlessly drive each of us every second of every day, the first two books revealed **16 secret keys** that drive what we do.

Books one and two also simplify and plainly explain not only *Body* and *Mind* (or **Soma** and **Cognitive**) integrations but also the **Inbound** and **Outbound** mechanisms and processes that enable survival, drive behaviours, formulate personality, enable awareness, facilitate conscious intervention and so much, much more.

Overview

A fundamental **Key** is that two types of Habits exist - **Soma-Habits** and **Cognitive-Habits**.

> Collectively called the **Habit-Duo**, they literally drive most of one's interactions with the **Out-There** - more than 95%. As **Self-Duo** Habits (Body-Self and Mind-Self) are so incredibly pervasive and rapid, they substantively define one's personality.

They spirit and are responsible for not only **Outbound** actions or movements that extensively define one's second-by-second physical existence but also thinking, speaking, perceptions and so forth. Furthermore, Book-one and Book-two proved that because of our extreme mobility, **Habitual-Preponderance** is essential for species survival.

In fact, if habits did not exist **DO**ing anything would be a massive chore. For instance, without Habits, just scratching your cheek would expend all ones cognitive processing resources for hours. Thus, one could neither accomplish any complex actions nor survive.

> To prove the enormity of the Habit gift, try to 'think' you way through each step involved in picking up a fork. Alternately, while driving to the store, record all the hundreds of calculations necessary to make just one left turn.

Even though the above calculations would be boggling to mentally figure out, write down and deploy, one's genetically provisioned Habits perform complex feats like these with ease, 24/7: such as, standing, sitting, walking, talking, thinking, etc., etc. Yes, speaking and thinking are Cognitive-Habits.

Without question then, Habitual contributions, form an enormous portion of our essential nature. So much so in fact, we could be considered (due to their persistent expertise) a Habitual-Species.

Within this framework, *Way Better* Your L.I.F.E^2. Book-two exposed how we **Solution** (i.e., **Figure-It-Out** and find **The-Ways**).

Progressing from the solid **How-We-Work** foundations of books one and two, **Tactics** (Book-three) provides easily useable deployment methodologies that WILL absolutely ensure you *Way Better* Your L.I.F.E^2.

Overview

The *Way Better* Your L.I.F.E². books progressively resolve many, many **How-We-Work** confusions: For instance, they clarify issues such as: how habits form (there are two types, not just one); why the **Habit-Duo** is so pervasive; how to engage **Habit-Power** to easily create new and significantly more beneficial **Pro-habits** and disarm addictions, destructive behaviours and the like; how to stop destructive **chaos-habits** from continuing to create you; how to inspire one's massive **Mind** or Cognitive arsenal at will; and so much, much more.

The first part of Book-three's subtitle, **Create Pro-habits that Get you What You TRULY Want** is intended to suggest that once **Habit-Power** is ramped-up, it will become your continuously vigilant and automated friend (as this is the nature of Habits) entirely focused on **fulfilling your wishes** and **your dreams**: Once you fully understand how Habit-Power functions, of course.

Stated differently, once the **23 secret keys** are grasped, you will be fully enabled to consciously choose and design your own Pro-habits that will strive automatically and relentlessly to *Way Better* Your L.I.F.E². by getting you what you **TRULY** want.

What could be better … really?

Interaction Opportunity:

The *Way Better* Your L.I.F.E². Trilogy is intended to inspire ongoing feedback: pros, cons, suggestions, additional detail, enhancements, etc.

In that regard, DavidHastingsTheAuthor@gmail.com is available for all to contribute what they will. For prompt response, please type **Tactics** (only please) in the subject line.

Additionally, watch for postings on social media sites where additional opportunities to provide your thoughts are available.

For my son Brandon,

As nothing is certain,
Everything is possible.

Action your day-dreams!

Remember to L.I.F.E^2:
Live in Full Experience and Excitement

Table of Contents

Preface

Transition

Tactics: Essentials

Wrap-Up

Diagrams

Preface

Why do not all possible ideas occur for everyone at conception or birth?

This is because throughout your lifetime, 100% of the varied information about what is going on **Out-There** must be gathered via a family of biological collectors called **sensory-arrays**.

> Undeniably, one's Deluge environment **24/7** randomly pummels or **Bombards** each of us with potentially catastrophic impact events from the **Out-There**.

Consequently, the only source of the action-potential building blocks or **fodder** that culminate in ideas, is **Deluge** or **Bombardment** events that have actually affected one's sensory event-horizons.

In other words, ideas only spawn from **fodder**, which is THE direct consequence of only those **Out-There** events, matter and light, which have literally 'collided' with our biology (i.e., our physical Soma or Body-Selves).

To clarify, think of your interaction with the Out-There this way. 'Stuff' or potential events (Deluge) are happening everywhere all the time. Regardless of your interaction with them due to proximity, this is so.

As you move around within your **Bombardment-Sphere**, you physically collide with ongoing events that are crossing your path. Stated differently, as you move about variously tuned sensory-receptors (sensory-neurons) are 'struck' by and consequently accept some of the Out-There activity.

However, due to the locations, sensitivities and varieties of sensory-arrays, (numbering in the many dozens), simply being 'struck' is not sufficient to spirit sensory-acceptance.

More specifically, **sensory-acceptance** means that one or more (Body-Self or Mind-Self) sensory-receptors has been first 'struck' by a Bombardment-Sphere event (be it smell, taste, touch, light, etc.) and then subsequently converted the mechanical energy of the Deluge-event into electrical energy (i.e., action-potential).

> See *Way Better* Your L.I.F.E^2.: **Body-Self** Detailed-Discussion section for complete terminology explanations.

Conversion

For sensory-receptors to accomplish 'conversion' into action-potential though, three other requirements must be fulfilled. First, the sensory event-horizon 'impact' area (or Location-ID) must have some sensory-neurons in ready-state. Second and third, the Deluge event must be not only frequency-appropriate (Tolerable-Signal) but also of sufficient intensity (Threshold-Potential).

Only when all conditions are met can a Deluge event be sensory-accepted, morphed, attenuated and transmitted onward toward applicable neural processors as action-potential.

Both notable and fundamental is that events or **Deluge** (sound, smell, taste, touch, vision, etc.), if they are to be 'noticed', must 'physically' contact one's biology. Specifically, the impact must occur on a single celled, frequency-particular structure called a **receptor-neuron**.

Thing is … a sensory-neuron is very, very small. Individually it is not able to provide sufficient outbound energy or **action-potential** to be 'noticed' by uplink cerebral processors.

Get Noticed

Fortunately, genetics provides solution by creating small, localized collections of sensory-neurons (what I term **Location-ID**'s) that can be simultaneously sensitive to the same very specific Deluge frequency.

In other words, sensory-array family members are identifiable by the frequency each sensory-neuron within their Location-ID group is genetically predisposed to accept.

Thus, the eyes don't hear and the ears don't see.

This **synchronistic-collaboration** strategy I coin **interlocatometry**, thus massively increases outbound action-potential signal density or resolution, which thereby has the potential to be 'noticed'.

Just to be clear, sensory-neurons are the initialization point for 100% of everything we now 'know' or will ever 'know'.

In other words, they and they alone are our interface to the **Out-There**. For future discussions, this fact, which may be startling to most, is extremely important to grasp.

Stated differently for clarity then, one's vast and varied networks of sensors are the initial touch-points that each, in the right conditions, sensory-accept a portion of their frequency-limited range of the Deluge that is pummelling you 24/7.

Like a vast array of radio-frequency parabolic collectors that (like the Very Large Array in New Mexico) are tuned to gather specific radio frequencies from space, our sensors similarly keep us apprised of what is going on **Out-There**.

However, rather than scanning the vastness of space our sensory-array receptors are sensitive to Deluge events within one's Bombardment-Sphere or nearby pool of potential impact-events.

Think of your individual Bombardment-Sphere as the enveloping external and/or internal environments, which produce events (like traffic noise, sunshine, rain, upset stomach, breathing, etc.) that have the potential to affect you.

Aside: It is my guess that the chaps who received the Nobel prize in 1946 had some inkling about how our physiology gathers signals from the vast Out-There. I suggest this because they introduced a concept called astronomical interferometry. The technique is all about increasing signal density when one antenna will not provide enough signal from space to be workable or 'noticed'.

Being 'noticed' was accomplished for them by coordinating a large number of parabolic antennas. When all are both 'collecting' from the 'same' spot within the vast extra-terrestrial **Out-There** and all tuned to accept the same frequency, they thus emulate a very, very large antenna.

> Signal combining thus yields signal of sufficient strength or density to be workable to receiving mechanisms (computers in today's world). For uncovering a universal strategy, which has been applied to many other scientific disciplines … Kudos to them!

Fodder

For us, sensory-acceptance and subsequent action-potential morphing and amalgamation into a **current-new** 'noticeable' data-stream literally provides 100% of one's information, fodder or **signal-flow**.

This is critical to grasp as it is the current-new action-potential that provisions 100% of the **fodder** with which corporeal **Inbound** neurological processing mechanisms have to work to enable everything we are and everything we do.

An incredibly beneficial outcome of brain-mass or cerebral processing is that most 'noticeable' current-new action-potential, originating from one's **Bombardment-Sphere** is captured and not lost.

> Specifically, current-new is retained in multiple and vast **data-archive** resources (neurological action-potential **data-storehouses**) as referenceable **archived-old**.

Think of **current-new** and **archived-old** as follows. When you want to use your cellphone, security requires you to enter a password: this action is marginally equivalent to sensory-acceptance of current-new. Once entered, cellphone software checks the password against its data-archive: this is similar to cerebral processor archived-old Recognition-Assessment.

> Even though password-acceptance and data-archive comparison are technologically very different to neurological systems, two outcomes are the same: the current-new (entered) password when compared to archived-old (stored password) is either recognized or **UN**-recognized and the result instigates pertinent and contiguous action.

Species Defining

Species defining is that we have been genetically gifted with not only extreme neurological capacity to store very granular action-potential frequencies or fodder but also with the capability to retrieve the particular **frequency-matched** archived-old fodder that is specifically pertinent to a current-new event.

Retrieval capability is phenomenal because it enables broad-scope **Recognition-Analysis**. Its rapid and finely honed processors comparatively-analyze **current-new** to either **archived-old same** (for Body-Self) or **significantly-similar** (for Mind-Self) to determine whether a current-new event is recognized or **UN**-recognized. This is excellent because it saves reinventing-the-wheel for repetitive Deluge events.

Critically therefore, as current-new and the effectiveness of its action-potential disposition in **data-archives** defines everything one is and everything one can become, the functioning of responsible **neural-mechanisms** is imperative to understand.

Body-Self

Thus, the first book, *Way Better* Your L.I.F.E^2.:~ **Body-Self** (aka **Soma-Self**) begins by clearly explaining all the fascinating How-We-Work stages or **Component** mechanisms and methodologies that are engaged by Body-Self (or just Body).

Component strategies progress from sensory-acceptance through multiple stages to culminate at **Soma-Actions** (see IS-101 and IS-102 illustrations near the end of the book or on-line).

> For Body-Self '**problematic**' issues (those it cannot completely handle: i.e., **UN**-recognized and/or high-intensity), **Body-Self** (aka Soma-Self) employs its **Cognitive-Alert** strategy, which is the only integration pathway to **Mind-Self** (aka Cognitive-Self or just Mind).

Thus, the Cognitive-Alert 'in-box' (Cluster-Works on the 'IS-103' diagram near the end of the book or on-line) is where *Way Better* Your L.I.F.E^2.: Mind-Self discussions begin.

Mind-Self

Book-two greatly expands one's understanding of How-We-Work by thoroughly explaining, among many other things, not only the progressive neuro-technology of **How-We-Think** but also Mind-Self's full-circle collaboration back to Body-Self.

Primarily, Mind-Self and its tremendous **Figure-It-Out** resource are all about **Solutioning**.

Mind-Self 'Solutions' by seeking answers for its created **Puzzles** (E-Puzzles) by not only retrieval from Mind-Self's multi-Tiered data-archives but also the issuance of **Test-Its**.

Test-It's are a fascinating strategy. **Figure-It-Out** formulates and deploys various intensities of Test-Its to instigate appropriate action-intensity physical (Body-Self) motions. Thus, Solutioning is accomplished via the gathering of additional sensory-information from **Out-There** thru cyclical sensory-feedback.

Mind-self, by additionally bringing its sensory-arrays on-line (vision) is able to Solution not only Body-Self's problematic issues but also in the right conditions, enable conscious thought, awareness and actions.

Figure-It-Out

Everyone is neurologically equipped to **Figure-It-Out**.

On one hand are arrays of sensory-equipment that feed the Solutioning process by being enabled to sensory-accept their restricted portion of the ongoing **Deluge** from the **Out-There**.

On the other hand are incredible processing and data-storehousing capabilities that are enabled to resolve and retain the copious amount of streaming **fodder**. These mechanisms rapidly filter and retain the copious granular frequency-aspects of a something's **current-new** facets (current sensory-accepted and morphed action-potential information) in magnificently designed **data-archives** (or action-potential neurological storehouses).

Action-potential collecting and **current-new** retention though would not be useful without higher-level genetically designed processors enabled to not only retrieve previously sensory-accepted and neurologically stored **archived-old** snippets from appropriate (i.e., correlated to current-new) data-archives but also deploy specific and appropriate actions to move us about within our **Bombardment-Spheres** and, when external conditions are threatening, quickly out of harm's way.

Fortuitously, both capacity to acquire granular aspects and capability to understand how something works have been genetically gifted to each of us.

Thus enabled, possibilities are endless: once one knows **How-We-Truly-Work** that is.

> Undeniable therefore, understanding **How-We-Work** (in lieu of guessing) is the vastly superior option that this series employs to *Way Better* Your L.I.F.E^2.

Stated differently, the profound benefit derived by learning **How-We-Work** is that 'random guessing' about one's **action-drivers** will be replaced by well-informed choice and option-based decisions.

Indeed, based on intimate familiarity with one's true functions and functionality (i.e., How-We-Work), actions will categorically be more accurate.

Excitingly then, once the aspects of How-We-Work are grasped, you will be completely enabled to easily *Way Better* Your L.I.F.E^2.

Some Trilogy Keys to date

Way Better Your L.I.F.E^2.: **Body** begins its journey by realigning one's understanding of the nature of the Deluge that is swirling around 24/7 in each of our **Bombardment-Spheres** (or surrounding physical environments).

Incredibly, all interfaces or event-horizon touch-points for first contact with the **Out-There** are provided by one's **sensory-arrays**.

Therefore, as sensory-arrays provision the first-contact points for 100% of one's lifetime experiences, sensory **event-horizons** are where clarification of **How-We-Work** commences.

Fortunately, although each millisecond millions of sensory-impact events are possible from the Out-There, a substantially smaller quantity are **sensory-accepted**.

Amazingly, sensory event-horizons are enabled to not only select and accept raw sensory information (current-new Deluge events) but also morph it into action-potential.

Action-potential is phenomenal because it is the **neurological-currency** or **fodder** upon whose foundation is established everything one currently is and 'knows' and everything one can become and will 'know'.

Amazingly, it is 'fodder' that is utilized to populate the many diverse **data-storehousing** neural-arrays that are dedicated to **data-archiving**.

In other words, one's astonishing array of sensory-systems, which are the initiation-points for all we know and all we can become, gather fodder 24/7, so **Self-Duo's** (Body and Mind) cerebral mechanisms can provide continuity - albeit differently - to what is going on **Out-There**.

Incredibly, sensory-event information, action-potential or **Tags**, when subsequently assembled and morphed into larger **Tag-Cluster** groupings by various arrays of brain-mass neural processors provision 100% of the 'larger' action-potential assemblies or **fodder**, which drive us every second of every day.

To summarize then, the first two *Way Better* Your L.I.F.E². books clearly and carefully detail conditions necessary for raw-data from **Out-There** to be accepted, then selectively assembled, morphed, processed and data-storehoused as **action-potentials** in **Body-Self** (or **Soma-Self**) neural real-estate and, if conditions are right, differently populate the many **Tiers** or data-archive layers of **Mind-Self** or **Cognitive-Self**.

Crucially, survival potential enhancement is also facilitated by neural-processors utilizing data-archived action-potentials for **Recognition-Analysis**.

The mandate of Recognition-Analysis is to determine the status of a sensory-accepted new Deluge event as either recognized or **UN**-recognized. It does this by comparing a **current-new** action-potential to a frequency congruent **archived-old** action-potential.

In other words, the first two books specify how ongoing new Deluge **fodder** is utilized to comparatively-analyze **current-new** to retrieved **archived-old** action-potentials.

Expansively, they also explained the extended magnitude of Recognition-Analysis: to enable cerebral neural-processors to instigate outbound responses that are both applicable and synchronous with ongoing current-new Deluge events.

Comprehensively, the first two books also explained how very precise collaborative interactions between **Body** (Soma) and **Mind** (Cognitive) provision not just survival but also, in the right conditions can spirit conscious awareness.

Way Better Your L.I.F.E^2.: **Tactics** builds upwards by detailing the Mind-Self functions that not only critically form the impetus for memory and recall but also importantly enable the improvement of one's **living-conditions**.

Engagingly, the Trilogy extends well beyond the mechanics of just data-acquisition and data-archiving though. Systematically, it also explains how action-potential comes to be utilized in the creation of memories, dreams, imagination, beliefs, behaviours, attitudes and much, much more.

Fantastically, and to everyone's great benefit, when **fodder** is manipulated and storehoused within **Mind-Self's** five-tier data-archive architecture, the multitudinous textures of each person's 'personality' is also forged.

Self-Duo's Habitual Arsenals

Automatically (i.e., without conscious intervention), Habits perform granular actions on your behalf every second of every day: In fact, Habitual 'behaviours' drive upwards of 95% of one's day.

Critically then, **fodder** storehousing has a paramount purpose: to enable rapid patterned habitual-responses to keep you safe by counterbalancing event-horizon current-new events.

Secondarily, but just as important, these second-by-second **habit-actioners** ensure smooth micro-motions so we do not physically 'jerk' through our day due to inconsistent outbound action directives.

Significantly, most habit-pattern driver set 'selections', from self-doubt to addictions and beyond were instilled by domesticators: i.e., not consciously chosen by you to benefit you.

Crucially, once you understand Habitual preponderance, its origins and one's – **Habit-Force** actioners, you will possess an essential clue to taking back your **Habit-Power**, so you can *Way Better* Your L.I.F.E[2]. by actually getting what you **TRULY** want.

Only when Habit-Power is being choicefully deployed can one create their own selected and far more useful Habitual-Responders.

In other words, possible absolutely is that everyone is easily capable of simultaneously creating self-designed **pro-habits** and stopping their old **chaos-habits** from creating them.

Deluge is pummelling one's sensory **event-horizons** 24/7.

Critical to understand however, is that it is only the sensory-accepted portions of the **Out-There** onslaught that determines all we are and all we can become.

This understanding is **Key** because interaction with the **Out-There** is only possible because of two fundamental and extraordinary genetically provisioned capabilities.

First, specialized neurons in cerebral brain-mass have been variously enabled to retain morphed action-potential (**fodder**) in multiple and functionally variant data-archives. Second, processors are empowered with the capability to retrieve and cross-compare **current-new** to **archived-old**.

The take-away then … one's surrounding physical conditions or **Bombardment-Sphere** environment is particularly significant (as it is the sole current-new and data-archive contributor) because changing its texture therefore has direct correlation to enhancing one's **living-experiences**.

In other words, by simply changing the content of Deluge events, one can influence, immediately and absolutely, not only current events and therefore **Body-Habit** and **Mind-Habit** actions but also cognitive **Experience-Sense** perceptions, attitudes, the **Way-We-Think** … and thus one's future direction!

It is easy to validate this statement: simply go for a massage when stressed. Both physical and mental responses will be substantially different. Transformations are a consequence of the dramatic change in sensory-acceptance because of the change in Bombardment-Sphere conditions being delivered to sensory-array event-horizons.

The existence of **habit-driven** auto-response patterns is significantly great news.

This is true because once aware of **How-We-Work** you can literally create more-useful **GO-TO** pro-habits by first adjusting your **Bombardment-Sphere** environment: And as a huge bonus thereby use the genetically provisioned **Habit-Power** to upgrade your performance, experiences, passions and **living-directions** as well!

Excitingly, by integrating the *Way Better* Your L.I.F.E². series **How-We-Work** concepts into your own data-archives, you will recognize not only the mechanisms behind data-acquisition foddering processes but also how sensory-acceptance and thus **fodder** can be adjusted to empower, take control of and truly create your own automatically driven pro-habit **living-outcomes** that will absolutely get you what you **TRULY** want!

Refresher: Books One and Two

In order to define **How-We-Work**, *Way Better* Your L.I.F.E².: **Body** (Book-one) begins with Body sensory origins. It travels the reader on four fun and informative virtual sojourns or journeys through many exciting **Body** or **Soma-Self** mechanisms that are dedicated to maximizing physical survival.

Initializing the series, the first *Way Better* Your L.I.F.E².: **Body-Self** journey propels the reader from the **Out-There** universe of incessant **Bombardment** or **Deluge** on event-horizons and through incredible sensory-acceptance strategies. **Body-Self** then follows the action-potential data-flow (morphed sensory-accepted information) through multiple Body-Self mechanisms to **Soma-Actions**, which provide one-half of the **Habit-Force** that facilitates our survival.

Incredibly, when sensory-accepted Bombardment (current-new) is **UN-recognized** and/or **sufficiently-intense** (thus **problematic** for Body-Self), Body-Self utilizes its 'Body-Self to Mind-Self' interface - the **Cognitive-Alert** - to request **Solutioning** assistance from **Mind-Self** (aka Cognitive-Self).

Consequently, *Way Better* Your L.I.F.E^2.: **Mind-Self** (book-two) picks-up where *Way Better* Your L.I.F.E^2.: **Body-Self** left-off: at the Mind-Self assistance-request **Cluster-Works in-box** for **problematic** issues.

Continuing onward, Book-two tours the reader through the many and varied mechanisms, constructs and **Mind-Self** processes, which, depending on the involved **Cognitive-Pathway**, drive awareness, thought, ingenuity and one's incredible capacity to **Solution** or **Figure-It-Out** and find **The-Ways**.

> Additionally, for the first time, *Way Better* Your L.I.F.E^2.: **Mind-Self** provides a giant leap in understanding **How-We-Work** by explaining **THE** vital or **Key** role the emotional **excitement-gradient** plays for not only data-storage and recall but also the creation of beliefs, personality, behaviour, **Cognitive-Habits** and so much more.

Five **Key** and fascinating **Cognitive-Pathway** journeys detail how **Figure-It-Out** is able to expedite **Solutioning**: even when sensory-events quickly escalate from **Nominal** to extremely intense.

Way Better Your L.I.F.E^2.: **Mind-Self** also details how **Figure-It-Out** operates to proactively find **The-Ways** (answers) for both short and extended-term questions or **Puzzles** that have three possible initiators: Body-Self **Soma-Sensors**, Mind-Self **Visual-Sensors** and cognitive positing by **Devise-Mulling's** intuitive processes.

> Powerfully, **Figure-It-Out's** extended capabilities enable it to utilize not just 'same' (as for Body-Self) but also **significantly-similar** fodder (archived-old) that it retrieves from data-archives to **answer** or **Solution** its **Puzzles**.

As **Solution** is being endeavoured, regardless of **Puzzle** origination, **Parameter-Processor** and possibly **Cognition-Complex** (when conditions are 'right') collaboratively tailor outbound-action-packet recommendations or **Test-Its**. Specifically purposed to spirit physical or Body-Self action, Test-Its thereby impel cyclical sensory-feedback from **Out-There**.

> Stated differently, in order to provide answers, multiple appropriate-to-puzzle (i.e., appropriate to current-new Deluge) Test-Its are designed to gather additional current-new from **Out-There** in an ongoing Feedback-Loop until Puzzle resolution is attained.

Thus, Test-Its play the reciprocal role of Body-Self-to-Mind-Self **Cognitive-Alerts**: i.e., Test-Its provide the sole outbound from **Mind-Self-to-Body-Self** interface. Thus, Test-Its are instrumental in provisioning **Figure-It-Out** with incremental **Solutions** or **answers** for its created **Puzzles** (questions).

> Incredible as well, in order to engage appropriate physical-responders that in turn **fodder** the **Feedback-Loop**, Test-Its are first sent to **Template-Component**. Thus, it exclusively provides the transition between one's **In-Here** 'systematized' cognitive-world and the **Out-There** chaos-world.

More specifically, Template-Component first morphs a Test-It data-packet to align with Cognitive-Pathway integrated current-new/archived-old data-flow and then sends its **Template-Packet** to **Response-Component** for final detailing of its Body-Self interfacing outbound configuration.

Whether utilizing an existing **Response-Pattern** or instigating the design of a new one, Test-It outbound action-packets synchronistically activate physical Soma or Body-Self structures (muscles, etc.), which successively realign position within one's **Bombardment-Sphere** and therefore not only propel one away from harm but also as a consequence of movement, gather feedback.

The second half of the **Habit-Force** dedicated to maximizing survival are **Cognitive-Habits**.

Thus, Cognitive-Habits not only significantly enhance one's Bombardment-Sphere **broader-scope** condition management but also moderate how one's Cognitive-Pathway outbounds, which provision the frequency-fodder for one's ongoing 'reality', i.e., the **Movie-of-Your-Life** is formulated, animated and delivered.

Way Better Your L.I.F.E².: **Tactics** purposefully applies the **How-We-Work** knowledge provided in both *Way Better* Your L.I.F.E².: **Body-Self** (Book-one) and *Way Better* Your L.I.F.E².: **Mind-Self** (Book-two) to greatly enhance one's practical day-to-day adventures or **L.I.F.E².**, which you may recall from the introduction is this author's acronym for Living-in-Full-Experience-and-Excitement.

Habit-Power drives most of one's day. Therefore, one of the many objectives of Book-three is to specify strategies to hone **Habit-Power** in order to not only **Create-New-Habits** (**pro**ductive or **pro-habits**) but also simultaneously stop **Your-Old-**

Habits (domesticated non-useful **chaos-habits** such as addictions, negative self-talk and the like (further detailed below) from **Creating-You**.

In this regard, **Tactics** will explain how to not only engage **Self-Duo** to mine **Habit-Power's** massive renewable resource but also exploit both **Self-Duo** and **Cognition-Complex** to better **Figure-It-Out** and find **The-Ways** to vastly more fulfilling outcomes.

> Book 3's subtitle, **Are You Creating Habits to Get What You TRULY Want** is intended to suggest that once **Habit-Power** is ramped-up, it will become your continuously vigilant and automated friend (as this is the nature of Habits), whose **Habit-Force** will be entirely focused on **fulfilling your wishes** and **your dreams**: Once you fully understand how it functions, of course.

Habit-Duo

The *Way Better* Your L.I.F.E^2. Trilogy was named as such for specific reasons. *Way Better* Your L.I.F.E^2.: **Body-Self** and *Way Better* Your L.I.F.E^2.: **Mind-Self** extensively defined both **Habit-Force** features and significances necessary for not only physically surviving but also enhancing one's **living-conditions**.

Thus, the first two books revealed many Habit benefits and characteristics: such as, their utility; origins; what conditions engage them; how they manifest; their key actioning triggers; their mechanisms of deployment; how they define how we roll; physiological interactions; and so on.

The first two books additionally proved that all data-archive populating could be traced back to an incredible variety of sensory-arrays, which accept a particular range or portion of the Deluge frequency-gradient.

> Interestingly, sensory-arrays are significantly alike for all members of our species and similar for other species as well.

Moreover, these books substantiated complex Harmonic data-archives, such as Habits, as well as all others are spirited from the specific information or **fodder**, which was sensory-accepted and in some cases, attenuated with frequency specific location identification data at each sensory-arrays event-horizon.

As well, they clearly established that Soma-Habits and Cognitive-Habits working together in concert (as the Habit-Duo), shape the critical **Habit-Force** actioning strategy for successfully surviving one's continuously **Bombarding** and potentially destructive environment.

These books clearly showed that by changing Deluge or more specifically by changing Bombardment-Sphere sensory-impacting events, one can create and make more useful not only Soma-Habits but also Cognitive-Habits such as beliefs, perspectives and a vast array of others.

This revelation is significant because this Key discloses an incredibly powerful design, which makes it possible to become anything you **TRULY** want to be and acquire any physical thing you **TRULY** want to have.

Habits: Friend or Foe

Actually, Habits can be either: it's up to you.

As you might recall, Body-Self (aka Soma-Self), while deploying **Soma-Habits** synchronously creates a tailored **Cognitive-Alert**, when a sensory-accepted event is **UN**-recognized and/or of higher-intensity.

These 'Body-Self-to-Mind-Self' Cognitive-Alert **data-packages** are individually tailored from current-new action-potential by Body-Self to request **Solutioning** assistance from **Mind-Self**.

> In other words, they interface by communicating current-new **problematic** Body-sensory issues (i.e., a sensory-accepted Soma-event that is **UN**-recognized and/or of higher-intensity).

Critically, Cognitive-Alerts that arrive at the Cognitive-Self **Cluster-Works** in-box are evaluated immediately.

After Cognitive-Self assessment, morphing and processing of the Cognitive-Alert, **Figure-It-Out** mechanisms, such as **Parameter-Processor** and **Cognition-Complex**, formulate and issue a variety of various intensity **Test-It** directives.

Test-Its are specifically formulated from both current-new and archived-old. They thus maximize safety and survival possibilities by spiriting **Body-Self** movements (improved positional changes) within one's **Bombardment-Sphere**.

Synchronously then, each of the Habit-Duo actioners, **Soma-Habits** and **Cognitive-Habits** provide one-half of the collaborative **Habit-Force** necessary to evade extinction and/or improve Bombardment-Sphere conditions.

Let's look at sensory-information from a different perspective.

Ever wonder how we come to know stuff: i.e., what provisions detailed recall; what mechanisms assimilate current-new sensory-accepted events with archived-old data-repositories (memory); why some of one's recall is easy and vivid, while some is difficult and vague; etc.?

Undeniably, if one could fully comprehend sensory-information origins, characteristics and data-flow through neurological systems as well as one's extraordinary processing capabilities, methodologies and structures, the usefulness of such knowledge would be enormous.

Understanding would be excellent as one would then be in an extremely strong position to create circumstances that would purposefully deliver fodder tailored to creating pro-habits to get what one **TRULY** wants.

> In that Habits are a major enabler of one's day-to-day survival and existence, it would also be useful to gain clarity about these amazing facilitators.

Classically, the definition of 'a habit' goes something like this: a habit is any automated behavior (auto-response) and/or function occurring with little or no awareness or (necessary) cognitive interception.

Contained within this definition, which at first seems simple and self-evident, are significant, perhaps unclear, fundamental concepts, which raise pertinent questions requiring clarification: Such as, what is a habit; what is auto-response; how can habits occur with little or no awareness; what is cognitive interception; how are habit and cognitive aspects related or interrelated?

Our current concept of a habit as a stand-alone process is utterly incorrect from any viewpoint: Neuro-physiologically; genetically; psychologically; etc. It is an old and outdated mono-dimensional and limiting concept. This is because originating thinkers attempted to explain human behaviour without substantial understanding of **How-We-Work**.

Although the classical habit definition, due to its vagueness and inaccuracy is not functional, there is no argument that biological or Body-Self auto-responses or Soma-Habits exist.

> Notably, from our Mind-Self (Cognitive-Self) perspective, vast numbers of biological auto-response events seem to occur spontaneously, without any need for awareness: such as, breathing, heartbeat, salivation, etc. Potential to significantly interface and directly override most of these is minimal.

Also, evident are cognitive auto-responses or what this author calls Cognitive-Habits. Most, upwards of 80% of Cognitive-Habit events, also seem to occur spontaneously.

> The difference being one can choose to become aware of most of them and perform radical and rapid adjustments: a few of these potentially aware events are walking, running, speaking, thinking, self-talk, etc.

Although some Cognitive-Habits may have been purposefully created, they now mostly run on autopilot: actions such as sitting down; picking up a fork; writing; reading; etc.

> Globally speaking, upwards of 95% of our daily repetitive actions are habitually driven by **Soma-Habits** and **Cognitive-Habits**, which together are called the **Habit-Duo**.

In all significant respects then, we are without doubt, a **Habitual Species**, mostly driven throughout our existence not by conscious choice but by intrinsic, pervasive auto-responder Habits, which are our deepest nature.

> **Habits**, with their ability to respond us to safety rapidly, have always been and will continue to be the pervasive **Power** driving our survival.

In other words, one survives and thrives because **Habit-Power** is inescapable.

Habit-Power

> Habits do not stand-alone but are as threads in a tightly woven fabric; pull on one thread and many others are variously stirred as well.

Incredibly, if one combined Soma-Habit and Cognitive-Habit output, this duo would account for 'mechanically' running most of one's 'normal' or uneventful day.

Resultantly, they represent not only THE focal survival control devices but also with a different spin, THE provisioner of our greatest advantage.

Why 'advantage', one might ask? After all, if most of our day is controlled by habitual-responses from Body-Self and/or Mind-Self, how can Habit-Duo also be 'THE provisioner of our greatest advantage'?

Let me suggest the following.

You are in possession of two very powerful mechanisms: Body-Self and Mind-Self. Up to this juncture, most have disregarded or been minimally aware of **Habit-Power**: i.e., how Habits harness neurological processes plus biological and physiological resources to get the job of surviving done.

Even though Habit-Duo is our most staunch ally and champions most of our daily action responses, most consider it inconsequential. We much prefer to think of ourselves as a cognitive species fully in control of all our actions.

We were never informed that **Habit-Duo** could be summoned to be our strongest supporter and seamlessly and easily fulfill all our hopes and dreams.

Habits are **The-River** in which we live, which drive us. Don't swim upstream against your river but instead flow with it: then thrive and enjoy.

The expectation, which everyone relies on to always work (although most again do not think of it in these terms) is practice. One knows if you practice repeatedly (repetition), your skills will improve: Incredibly importantly though, only in relation to your interest or passion in acquiring the target skill-set of course.

To be clear then, practice is actually you creating Soma-Habits and Cognitive-Habits purposed for getting you what you truly want. Big exclamation point and bold **underline**: get you what you **TRULY** want; not what you think you might sort-of want.

Success of whatever nature is theoretically easy: create useful '**pro**-ductive' or **pro-habits** that support a good and healthy self-concept, drop them into your **habit-river** and then without work watch them get you what you TRULY want.

Alternately, **chaos-habits** like negative self-talk, which never allows you to congratulate yourself for progress will try to drive you up-river against the flow.

Trust me; the up-river direction will cause you a lot of work, effort and anguish.

> Fighting the **habit-current** will not only get you nowhere but also require you to be continually battling the **current** going very strongly against you in the other direction.

How powerful would you be if you could switch say 30% of your chaos-habits over to the pro-habit camp? What excitement you would have as your pro-habits seamlessly work to get you what you TRULY want.

Thus, one primary *Way Better* Your L.I.F.E².: **Tactics** mandate is to explain how to apply the extraordinary characteristics of Body-Self's and Mind-Self's many driving elements to create pro-habits and disengage chaos-habits and thus massively enhance one's living-experiences.

Think of the **Habit-Duo** as your very own

Dream Fulfillment Team

Make no mistake though: Habit-Duo is a colossal genetic gift provided to everyone without exception.

Why create your own pro-habits?

They will automatically and effortlessly (that is their inherent design) deliver all your dreams and desires once you fully understand how Body-Self and Mind-Self work individually and in harmony.

> Once aware, one can even turn Habit-Duo's power up to high … or at least up a few notches.

One more thing … do not waste any energy or time on trying to change or erase your malfunctioning **chaos-habits**: This is a neurophysiological impossibility!

> This is so because action-potential **fodder** has been packing multitudes of their Matched-Base-Frequency data-storehouse neurons for years and even decades. Their massive accumulation thus ensures they are the **GO-TO** responders for frequency 'matched' events: at least until you intercede and create alternate pro-habits.

In other words, the incredibly great news is that you can simply bypass chaos-habits and create your very own new, more useful and larger action-potential **pro-habits** from new information and choice.

Once accomplished … voila … they become the **GO-TO**'s instead.

> In other words, they become the ones working 24/7 … this time though … getting you what you **TRULY** want!

Actually, you can even begin to create pro-habits when you daydream and night dream about how your **living-experience** can and will change when **DO**ing what you passionately desire?

Without doubt then, we are a Habitual Species: mostly driven by intrinsic auto-responders that are our deepest nature.

> Why are we designed this way? What evolutionary selectors supported the continuance of this core habit feature? What purpose do auto-responders serve, if any? Can we upgrade some auto-responders to create lives bursting with richness? How do we live our lives more **Choice-Fully**? When do we feel most alive?

Way Better Your L.I.F.E^2.: **Tactics** will explore and answer these and other significant questions to enable your wildest dreams to become your **living-reality**!

> In addition, our habitual species predisposition is going to be viewed as a stellar feature not a handicap.

With this perspective, you can purposely create pro-habits that enable you to develop excellent relationships, create health and attain financial and spiritual riches. These exist all around you anyway: so is it not time to create pro-habits that will get you your fair share?

Let's be clear: **You do not have to be your chaos-habits**!

Realize that Habits, no matter how pervasive are only a basic survival building block. Even though behaviors are mostly dictated by your habitual responses, **everyone has a trump card**.

Remarkably, you are already enabled to not only create your own super-useful pro-habits but also simultaneously relegate the troublesome chaos-habits to oblivion!

What chaos-habits are we targeting?

You are going to create new pro-habits. Some you may never have even conceived possible: Pro-habits that will positively transform your way of thinking and thus your living-experiences.

In other words, we are going to identify chaos-habits that are holding you in place, create benefactor **GO-TO** pro-habits and simultaneously bypass their chaos-habit antagonists.

I can honestly say that I am a good person
with good intentions.

It's just my chaos-habits that keep messing me and others around!

As this is the case for so many, we are going to find the chaos-habits that do not serve, document them and define the shape of new and useful pro-habit **Butlers** that will enfranchise rather than disenfranchise one's desires.

You will transform into an enthralling **You-Force** of your choosing and become a new, integrated, aware, clear and powerful you.

The pro-habit creation process is not a trick or manipulation: the Habit-Duo is real. You will not be employing techniques or any external set of rules that need memorizing.

The pro-habit formation methodologies work by application of consistent principles, which **Tactics** will continue to expose and clarify.

Pro-habit creation will occur due to getting answers that provide accurate information to significant age-old questions about what we are, **How-We-Work** and more expansively, why we are here in this universe.

Way Better Your L.I.F.E^2.: **Tactics** first task is to uncover the 'dots' and then draw the lines between the dots for you.

This process will effectively not only expose the true picture of **How-We-Work** but also allay the misleading story all been systematically brainwashed to believe throughout the past three or more millennia: that you are not worthy and dream fulfillment is not possible for you.

Brainwash

Blinkers or blinders are still in use today. Horse handlers will tell you these vision restrictors or vision range limiters are used to keep the animal from being distracted or scared.

> This of course is a deception. The blinkers have almost nothing to do with the horse and most everything to do with the handler. The handler simply found a way to get his own way with the animal and have full power over it. The handler is happy when the horse does what he wants and is displeased when the horse does what it wants.

For thousands of years, in order to advantage and sustain itself, State in concert with Church, I am going to call these self-appointed, self-serving groups the **Beguilers** orchestrated its 'will' in such a way as to put blinkers on the populaces free thinking.

The Beguilers continual application of power by overwhelming slyness enabled the State/Church to change the very nature of the way 'the subjects' (all those but the most elite) thought: from freedom of thought through adherence to contrived rules.

A most devastating brainwash by 'State' Beguilers was achieving obedience through tyranny (arbitrary and uncontrolled application of power).

Beguilers knew, if the populace was forced to work at menial tasks 14 hours a day just to survive, kept in continual states of unrest and conflict with neighbors, and punished with horrifically brutal tortures of family and friends, there would simply be no time or inclination for an uprising.

Religious based Beguilers conjured an additional controlling deception. It was delivered in a manipulative dichotomy: obey and go to heaven; or disobey and go to hell.

The populace of many millennia was not privileged with education so had no idea of this fundamental falsification.

Possibly, we would have had a less bloody history if people had known that heaven and hell were given purposefully contrived meanings as places: instead of their most likely Aramaic translations where heaven means higher consciousness and hell, ignorance.

All understanding is already within both your capability and your reach.

My mandate is to expose How-We-Work so you have **personal-power** for the rest of your life. There will be no holding back or pointing you to other materials: this is the source and everything is included that is needed to transfer control to you. I want you to live in full experience and excitement (coined **L.I.F.E².**): Not in a year or more, but right now.

You can easily learn to countermand existing destructive and non-useful chaos-habits while creating automated pro-habit servants that create wealth, health and excellent relationships - especially with yourself.

If it's joy and fulfillment you have been seeking ... keep reading.

I would like one agreement from you though, which is within everyone's power to fulfill. Only start to read *Way Better* Your L.I.F.E.²: **Tactics** when you can complete it in 14 days.

I am serious about this because **The-Way-We-Think**, discussed later is our worst habit that enfolds a worst chaos-habit offender: procrastination. Thus, this is your first commitment exercise.

Significantly, Intention has no power (sorry Wayne) but **DO**ing absolutely does.

Self-Concept rule number one and two:

Only say what you can do … and then **DO** it 100%.

Transition

Firstly, I know some parts of the first two books were a bit of a tough read. Several PhD friends, although impressed with the unique content were quick to underscore this point. Subsequently, *Way Better* Your L.I.F.E².: **Tactics** will be more conversational than technical.

In support of a less technical, more conversational format, **Tactics** narrative will be minimally interrupted with concept re-explanations from books one and two: *Way Better* Your L.I.F.E².: **Body-Self** and *Way Better* Your L.I.F.E².: **Mind-Self**.

Instead, sections in the first two books will be offered for review when their perusing seems appropriate. Thus, if possible, keep them handy.

Furthermore, whereas books one and two were designed to explain the mechanics of **How-We-Work** within the Body-Self and Mind-Self frameworks, **Tactics** instead will expand upon their provided knowledge and instruct how to enhance one's living-conditions… massively.

Specifically, **Tactics** will focus directly on not only how to create '**pro**ductive' or **pro-habits** to get you what you **TRULY** want but also how to supersede not-useful **chaos-habits** such as addictions, disruptive behaviours, compulsions and so forth.

No question, **Habit-Duo** (Soma-Habits and Cognitive-Habits),
with its automated **Habit-Power** drivers action about
95% of one's 'normal' or unexceptional day.

Habitual Predominance

Habitual prevalence or **Habit-Force** is a very good thing when it both **gets** you what you **TRULY** want and additionally enables you to **know** what you **TRULY** want …undeniably even better.

However, when Habits are destructive to your potential and/or they barricade your passions from view, as is the case for compulsions, damaging responses, self-doubt, anger, reclusive behaviours, hiding, etc., then these **chaos-habits** would best be superseded by new, more useful and user friendly **pro-habits**.

Most second-by-second tenacious negative chaos-habit instigators were mostly created by domestication. This is significant because once one knows something's origination point, it is easy to travel to its source-point and interrupt its dominance.

Just as with the 'blinkers' discussion above, domestication was mostly for the benefit of others: for their control and comfort, not yours.

Resultantly, the concocted rules of others stifled your creativity and disallowed excited experimentation and inquisitive discovery: Much more the 'sit down and behave' command, than go, be free and explore scenario.

As a direct consequence, the seen-and-not-heard confining attitude of young-life influencers thus contributed significantly to severely limit self-expression and thus kept you from standing out in the crowd.

> In other words, domestication stifled by creating self-doubt chaos-habit habitual-responses, which kept doubting your decisions and being vanilla.

The exciting good news is that if you want your **living-experience** to be upgraded to awesome you can create new pro-habits by choice; utilizing new information gathered from new Bombardment-Sphere environments. By so doing, non-useful old chaos-habits can be effectively usurped.

One primary **Tactics** focus therefore is to explain methodologies to accomplish this transition.

Excitingly, new pro-habit design incorporates an incredible feature: once created they will continue working 24/7 without your having to toil hard (or at all actually) to manage them.

Significantly then, **Habitual-persistence** is a major bonus especially when pro-habits are getting you what you TRULY want.

Stubbornly though, chaos-habits created in the young years, even if detrimental to living the life you truly want, also work continuously.

This is an issue especially with the very worst central debilitator: self-doubt.

Self-doubt, which belongs to the **Way-We-Think** set of chaos-habits, is by far the worst of the destructive chaos-habits: They will be discussed a little further along.

Unfortunately, chaos-habits have been hardened by decades of sensory-accepted **fodder** from the **Out-There** populating myriads of Body-Self and Mind-Self data-archives.

Why is it so hard to break a habit?

Because you can't: Head-on, one can neither significantly change nor get rid of old habits.

Absolutely, this is a neurological impossibility because Habit action-potentials have been (and are being) stockpiled across multiple data-archives for almost as long as you've been alive.

So do not waste any time or energy on trying to do that!

However, one can successfully supersede or usurp a chaos-habit.

Fortunately, 'usurping' by creating a new pro-habit is not only easily workable but also much, much, much easier to **DO** than the **fruitless alternative** of trying to change a chaos-habit.

Nicely, creating pro-habits is fairly straightforward. Once created, it is simply a matter of exercising the new pro-habit until it furnishes sufficiently greater action-potential to become the **GO-TO** instead.

Additionally auspicious however is that once sufficient data-archive population is accomplished via new sensory-acceptance, new pro-habits will usurp domesticated chaos-habit influence and the pro-habit will be instilled as the **GO-TO** Habit-Force driver instead.

This is such great news it bears restating. When successfully created and filled-out with sufficient **fodder**, pro-habits will become the **GO-TO**'s, fully automated of course - as this is their nature - to get you the good stuff you **TRULY** want and not what someone else decided in your preteens and teens (and perhaps right now) was 'right' for you.

Remember … old chaos-habits do not ever, ever, ever just go away.

However, by not actuating them through use, some of their neural real-estate will be recycled and used for new pro-habits: definitely another big benefit of relegating chaos-habits toward well-deserved oblivion.

Habits are Focal

Habits are a major focus of **Tactics** because as we know **Habit-Power** drives the majority of one's 'normal' day.

Therefore, Book-three details strategies to hone **Habit-Power** for the purpose of creating pro-habits and disengaging chaos-habits.

In other words, by examining and understanding how Habit-Power **significances** are created, which drives each of us; it will be possible to create and engage more useful pro-habits and minimize the effects of destructive chaos-habits.

Expansively, *Way Better* Your L.I.F.E^2.: **Tactics** is purposed to explain not only how to **Create-New-Habits** (pro-habits) but also powerful strategies, which will assist in both actualizing your full potential and stop **Your-Old-Habits** (domesticated destructive chaos-habits) from continuing to **Create-You**.

As we now know several critical components, regarding the current state of Cognitive-Habits, let's be totally clear about their origins so pro-habit creation is unencumbered by vagueness.

As sensory-apparatus is the only **fodder** generator, critical to understand about the Habit formation process is that all new pro-habits and all old chaos-habits were by default formed from action-potential and subsequently fodder created immediately after an event was sensory-accepted.

In other words, both pro-habits and chaos-habits are formed **only** from the action-potentials or fodder of sensory-accepted events.

> Consequently, whatever one is exposed to (i.e., has experience with) will have implications within multiple data-archives and thus Habits.

Therefore, either a current-sensory-accepted event action-potential will be added to existing frequency-matched data-archive caches or the action-potential will create a new frequency-matched repository sect.

Recall that there are five Tiers of Cognitive data-archives, which are accumulating action-potentials within either frequency matched or sufficiently-similar caches or sects.

Also, recall that the higher the Cognitive-Self **Tier**, the more resistant to change it is. This is because potentially tens-of-thousands or more action-potential additions have foddered not only them but also all the interactive lower Tier sects as well.

> This means by the time we are 5 or 6 years young, many of one's Tier-5 Experience-Senses are already the action dictating **GO-TO**'s.

I you are in doubt about this, just ask a 5 year old their opinion about munching raw broccoli, especially when their exposure (sensory-acceptance) regarding its consumption has been minimal.

Invariably you will run into such huge resistance, you will quickly break out the diet they are used-to instead. 'Used-to' means their Experience-Sense or Cognitive-Habit regarding food acceptability is already strongly established.

Test-It Fodder 'Requestors'

Even though both Soma- Habits and Cognitive-Habits are definitely foddered by **inbound** action-potentials, extremely powerful Cognitive **Test-Its** (written as such is meant to include the five variations of Test-Its) players are perpetually at work as well.

As these multiple Test-It 'players' primary purpose is to provide **outbound** action-requests that are intensity proportionate to current-new, they are incredibly significant.

In other words, Test-Its are formulated to spirit adjustment to one's position within one's Bombardment-Sphere in proportion with Deluge intensity and location-ID(s); and therefore, they additionally determine the type of additional current-new **fodder** to be collected.

> Multiple Test-It 'players' are significant as their primary purpose is to provide **outbound** action-requests that are intensity proportionate to current-new.

Although Parameter-Processors Test-its and Delving-Trios Targeted, Ranged and Extensive-Delving **Test**-it, **TEST**-it and **TEST-IT**s (listed respectively) accommodate for escalation of intensity by formulating ever more complex outbounds, it is Devise-Mulling **Test-IT**'s, which have veto power.

> Obviously if one received negligible Deluge on sensory event-horizons, it would preclude any need for evaluation.

Here is a simple example of Test-Its at work. You are hungry. Well intentioned to buy some healthful fixings for a meal, you head to your favorite grocery store (all Test-It driven).

On the way however, you pass by for your favorite take-out and notice someone dressed as a big chicken holding a 50% off sign.

Due to the higher-intensity of both your hunger and the discount, Devise-Mulling kicks in and compel a series of **Test-IT**s that make your mouth water.

Synchronously, Devise-Mulling taps into your frequency appropriate Experience-Sense caches and presents not only an appealing virtual mental picture but also fires

Test-ITs that inspire you to drive in: even though Devise-Mulling is also telling you it's not a healthy choice.

The higher energy **GO-TO** junk-food wanting Cognitive chaos-habit wins out though as your frequenting the place has built appropriate data-archive caches with greater action-potentials; whereas the pro-habits pertaining to healthy-eating are less populated.

So, the first step to creating and enabling pro-habit power is to clearly understand the process of interrupting your chaos-habits.

First and foremost: control your exposure to tempting events by avoiding as many compromising sensory-impact (Deluge) factors as possible.

In other words, one choice that would have immediate positive repercussions is to change your path to the grocery store (i.e., your Bombardment-Sphere environment), so your route does not pass-by temptation.

Notably, Devise-Mulling **Test-IT**s are more powerful than the other Test-Its because Devise-Mulling taps into and incorporates Tier-5 Experience-Senses or Cognitive-Habits (like desires), which filter-out other options by deploying veto **Test-IT**s. More on this as we proceed.

So, while creating pro-habits and usurping chaos-habits, it will be necessary to make Bombardment-Sphere adjustments to not only enable new information and therefore upgraded Test-Its but also avoid habitually-triggerable external conditions and therefore chaos-habit generated **Test-IT**s.

Before continuing, a quick summary of the first two books touch-points has been compiled below to ensure clarity about How-We-Work. Please bookmark this page for easy reference.

Book-one and Book-two Underpinnings

A compilation of the principles and concepts established in *Way Better* Your L.I.F.E^2.: **Body-Self** and *Way Better* Your L.I.F.E^2.: **Mind-Self** is provided below. Its purpose is to assist in clarification of underlying principles as **Tactics** are presented.

Applicable Overall

Frequency is the basis upon which everything in the universe operates.

> This includes us as well because we are not separate but encapsulated within the laws of the universe.

Only frequencies (Deluge) within one's Bombardment-Sphere that reach sensory event-horizons have the potential to be sensory-accepted and incorporated into current evaluations and neural-archives as fodder.

Sensory-arrays manage Deluge frequency data; whereas neural processing systems manage action-potentials and fodder.

Processing systems both archive and retrieve by the universe standard: Frequency.

> Just as the universe utilizes frequency to immutably define every energy and matter bit, so do we utilize frequency for sensory-acceptance, comparison, sensory-event storage and recall. In other words, **frequency** is our **neurological currency**.

Body/Soma-Self

Only when the following three conditions are satisfied will frequency-based mechanical energy, bombarding Soma-sensory event-horizon sensory-neurons, be accepted: sensory-neurons must be in **ready-state**; when frequency is within a sensory-neurons range-of-acceptance (**Tolerable-Signal**); and signal or Bombardment strength is of sufficient intensity (**Threshold-Potential**) to activate a sensor-neuron.

While being converted into **action-potential** format, which is the standard 'language' or **currency** of post-acceptance neural functioning, many Soma sensory-accepted events or **SSAE's** are augmented by the application of frequency specific acceptance-site location identifiers or SLIDs (Soma Location-IDs).

Such enhancement ensures accurate recall of the impact site event: i.e., where you were touched and how hard; the direction of the noise and how loud; etc.

After acceptance, transport to brain processors and amalgamation with same frequencies within a short **Time-Stamp** interval, SSAE's (now **Tag-Cluster** action-potentials) are immediately frequency compared to applicable **data-archives** (i.e., **current-new** to **archived-old**) in order to determine if the current event is a re-occurrence (recognized) or new (UN-recognized).

Current-new to archived-old assessment is critical as its evaluation governs next steps.

When re-occurrence is established **recognized** event action-potentials increment or increase the overall action-potential intensity of the events **Matched-Base-Frequency**: i.e., a frequency compatible Bracket or data-archive.

'Size' or **intensity** does matter as it makes a higher-intensity Matched-Base-Frequency more dominant upon recall.

This is a major reason why either familiarity with a topic and/or intense exposure to closely similar events makes a Bracket the **GO-TO** when remembering. Resultantly, **exciting** is always easier to recall than mundane.

Many different frequency action-potentials (different Tag-Clusters) within a specific 'Time-Stamp' or common timeframe are utilized to form broad-scope **Harmonic** data-archives. These are fundamental to creating patterns, which in turn dictate Soma-Self or biological responses and furthermore accumulate to form **Soma-Habits**.

Soma sensory-accepted events or **SSAE's** when either **UN**-recognized and/or high-intensity additionally create an information **package** called a **Cognitive-Alert**, which distinctly notifies Cognitive-Self of a **problematic** event.

Mind/Cognitive-Self

Cooperatively, Cognitive-Self utilizes the Soma-Self provided Cognitive-Alert as an **action-flag** to bring its own **Cognitive-Sensor** array (vision) to bear on the problematic issue (in most cases).

Integration of pertinent visual and Cognitive-Alert data is accomplished by **Cross-Sensory-Bundling**. It utilizes a cross-comparison data-archive to 'match' **Visual Location IDentifiers** (VLID's) from the retinal grid to Soma location-identifiers (SLID's).

> With exposure, as one physically matures, cross-comparison data-archive connections evolve between VLIDs and SLIDs. These are maintained in visual cortex **Brackets** or data-archives. In this way, for instance, one 'recalls' the Soma-location to look at where touched.

Intensity (Tag-Cluster 'size' or action-potential) delivered by a Cognitive-Alert and/or incremented by Cross-Sensory-Bundling matching Cognitive-Sensor comparators (Visual) is critical in determining one of five (5) **Cognitive-Pathway** (CP) 'directions': from CP-1, which processes highest intensity survival events to CP-5 which manages lowest intensity.

Subsequently, **Matched** and/or high-intensity gets shuttled to **PRIORITY** channel, which can enable CP-3, CP-2 or CP-1 (upon follow-on evaluation); whereas **UN-matched** and/or low-intensity gets directed to **NORM** channel, which can enable either CP-4 or CP-5 (also upon further evaluation).

> Pertinently, only CP-3, CP-2 and/or CP-1 can engage Cognitive-Sensors (vision).

Cognitive-Pathways CP-4, CP-3, CP-2 and CP-1, which are within the bounds of the **Figure-It-Out Module**, create or augment two types of Cognitive-Self data-archives for inbound events within **Data-Matrix**: **Experiential-Accrual** (EA) and **Information-Assembly** (IA).

> The EA **harmonic-archive** is utilized to target similar events whereas IA provides the associated relevant event details.

The-Ways

When an event is **UN**-recognized, a **Puzzle** or **CP-Set** data-structure (formed from a single E-Puzzle and its many corresponding F-Puzzles) is created so Figure-It-Out ("It" being the problematic issue to be **Solutioned**) can resolve the issue and find **The-Ways**.

> Alternately, when an E-Puzzle already exists, appropriate CP-Set F-Puzzles are updated: also for Solutioning purposes.

Regardless of intensity, and upon notification from **Resolution-Processor** but after CP-Set interface, all Soma-Self action-potentials are first handled by **Parameter-Processor** to ensure fluid or uninterrupted physical movement.

> Parameter-Processor provides its own specific less-complex variety of Test-its, which are responsible for tiny transitional physical adjustments.

Cognition-Complex's **Delving-Trio** only engage to assist in 'Figuring-It-Out' when Parameter-Processor evaluates a CP-3, CP-2 or CP-1 intensity, which thus exceeds its limited handling range.

> Depending on intensity then, Delving-Trio capabilities enable three levels of upward cascading escalation progressing from **Targeted-Delving** to **Ranged-Delving** to **Extensive-Delving**.

In order to both coordinate escalation and create appropriately balanced (to current-events) response, Delving-Trio utilizes a temporary, specialized exclusive proprietary data-resource called **PT-assembly**.

> 'Appropriate balanced response' or Soma-Self actioning is implemented by the creation of up to three escalation levels of **Test-Its** or directives: **Test**-it; **TEST**-it; and **TEST-IT**, respectively.

Specifically, Test-It sequences (in **proportional increments** and in balance to a current-event) have specific purpose. They ameliorate the 'problematic' issue through cyclical sensory-feedback by suggesting Bombardment-Sphere physical body movements.

'Proportional increments' are represented to complement the engaged 'Pathway' on the **Cognitive-Pathways Model** diagram as Standard, Considered, Enhanced and SURVIVAL-responses.

Successively, **Template-Component** accepts and integrates Test-Its and creates repeatable response-patterns integrated and balanced to ongoing events to ensure rapid and accurate actions coordinated to received Test-Its.

Cognition-Complex additionally provisions **Devise-Mulling** that is the arena for conscious awareness and 'intuition'. Devise-Mulling always initiates when intensity of an unfolding event is sufficient to alert it.

However, three Devise-Mulling activators are possible: instigation by Body-Self Cognitive-Alerts triggering Visual-Sensors; Visual-Sensor processors proactively assessing a potentially harmful **remarkable-feature**; or its independent **Mulling**, ferreting or 'spontaneous thought' nature that creates 'Puzzles' for resolution.

Devise-Mulling provisions not only various levels of conscious awareness but also encompasses its own dedicated **DM-Assembly** data-resource, which is utilized to compile 'Mulled' information and create both CP-Sets (Puzzles) and its own complex variety of **Test-IT**s.

Devise-Mulling not only incorporates Cognitive-Habits or **Experience-Senses** (C-Cluster) when creating **Test-It**s but also is the arena for thinking, speaking, and so much more.

The-Movie-of-Your-Life

As beliefs, behaviors, personality et al are 100% compiled from sensory-acceptance roots; and in that vision is the only Cognitive-Sense; and in that awareness is a Cognitive-Self manifestation; it stands to 'reason' one's reality be presented as a visual mosaic by Mind-Self.

Only Mind-Self has the processing power to ensure one's individualized representation of reality or **The-Movie-of-Your-Life** is contiguous and continuous without blank spots … as anything less would be survival disastrous.

Tactics:

Essentials

Tactics will continue to explore and discuss both Habits and Test-Its. Why the Habit focus… so you can get control of your most powerful driver: **Habit-Power**? Why the Test-It focus… so you can intercede to spirit superior retrieved fodder that will greatly assist in getting you what you TRULY want?

The first two *Way Better* Your L.I.F.E^2. books established that the **Habit-Duo** (Soma-Self/Cognitive-Self) variously deploy **Habit-Force** to drive upwards of 95% of one's 'normal' or unremarkable day. They also underlined that Mind-Self, when Deluge is either UN-recognized and/or of higher-intensity, significantly influences Body-Self movements by issuing various complexities of Test-Its.

Without question, when sensory-redundancy fills one's day, habits operate automatically. Specifically, Soma-habits deploy in the routine of 'recognized' and low-intensity events and Cognitive-Habits activate not only in UN-recognized and elevated-intensity events but also in either recognized and slightly elevated-intensity events or UN-recognized and low-intensity events.

> The conclusion was clear. As 'Habit' expressions are responsible for most living-conditions, it would be prudent to create new automatic pro-habits to get what you **TRULY** want.

Furthermore, the first two books revealed that everything you are and everything you can become, from habitual-responses to beliefs and behaviors have their origin with the many types of Bombardment-Sphere pummelling Deluge (taste; touch; vision; etc.) being filtered then sensory-accepted at the event-horizons of an incredible array of sensory-receptors.

In other words, sensory-accepted Deluge alone is the start-point that actualizes Habit-Duo (i.e., Cognitive-Habits and Soma-Habits) as well as a broad array of data-archives and processing functions.

Tactics, by building upon **How-We-Work** foundations detailed in the first two books will provide specific tools that enable **pro-habit** creation: those you design by choice to get you what you **TRULY** want.

More specifically **Tactics** will detail what habits are; where they come from; their uses; their upsides and downsides; etc.

Tactics will delve deeply into not only specific ways to create new pro-habits that are more useful but also what actions are necessary and needed to eliminate self-destructive, addictive and less-useful **chaos-habits**: and thus their associated destructive Habitual patterned responses or detrimental outbound consequences, which others view as behaviours.

Additionally, **Tactics** will teach you how to enhance existing useful pro-habits and even put them on the fast track. For-instance, as living-conditions are significantly influenced or driven by the set of 'how you truly think about you' Cognitive-Habits or Experience-Senses, which most keep private, these will be targeted as well.

Living-Conditions

Whether the thousands and thousands of few millisecond duration miniscule Deluge feedback activities execute seemingly independently, like the habitual-actions of picking up a fork or coordinate into longer sequenced groupings, like using a variety of utensils to eat a meal, sensory-accepted events accrue to shape one's second-by-second, hourly, daily and lifetime **living-conditions** by forming Soma-Self and Cognitive-Self automated habits.

Clearly, even if one attempted to analyze some repetitive action series, i.e. one performed without thinking about each miniscule step, like the **Habit-Pattern** of brushing your teeth for instance, it would be difficult to reveal either habitual origins or its many seamless interactive components.

Bombardment Influence

Although we create attitudes, beliefs and significances in our lives,
they do not manifest independently:

In fact, they are the direct consequence of sensory-accepted
Bombardments from the **Out-There**
being sensory-accepted then retained as action-potentials
within arrays of data-archives.

The statement above underlines several facts, which are essential to understand if one is to create pro-habits successfully.

As a fundamental understanding and critical to appreciate is that all external and internal sensory event-horizon (tens-of-thousands of them) are being unrelentingly assaulted every millisecond (one, one thousands of a second) of every day by countless miniscule events from the Out-There: i.e., one-thousand Bombardment events per second per sensory-acceptance site or location-ID.

Just to refresh, 'Out-There' means external to the neural mechanisms that are responsible for data transmission as well as processing, creating and updating Soma-Self and Cognitive-Self data-archives and subsequently habit-patterns.

Secondly, stoking individual attitude and perceptual differences are the actions one performs every second of every day.

Significantly, the myriads of Bombardment-Sphere positional changes are the culprits that dramatically increase the Bombardment or Deluge variability with which the sensory-apparatus must cope.

In other words, it is continual slight to massive habitual and Test-It Bombardment-Sphere adjustments spawned as a consequence of our remarkable mobility, which vary the granularity of the millisecond-by-millisecond bombardment events pounding on each person's sensory event-horizons.

Pointedly then, it is sensory receptor neurons that singularly form the initialization-point or touch-point for not only short term behaviors, like taking a step but also copious data-archive foddering, which drives beliefs, attitudes and consistent behaviours like thinking, speaking, biases, attitudes and so forth.

Sensory Apparatus

From a neuro-physiological perspective, it would be overwhelming for both sensory-receptor neurons and brain-mass processors, if one's sensory equipment admitted all Universe-H Deluge without restriction.

Fortunately, sensory neurons are inherently frequency selective, which consequently results in much smaller portions of Bombardment being sensory-accepted.

> To review, please reread the detailed discussion section on **The Senses** (DD-001) in *Way Better* Your L.I.F.E^2.: **Body,** especially the 'Active', 'Tolerable-Signal' and 'Threshold-Potential' subsections.

Deliberately therefore, only sensory-accepted Deluge populates the data-archives that everyone subsequently relies on to **uniquely** evaluate current events.

> As we have learned, 'evaluation' is a benchmark neural-methodology whose frequency comparative process always assesses **current-new** event flow to retrieved **archived-old**.

Why 'uniquely': because data-archives will always be different between people?

Person-to-person variances are due to not only differing Deluge sensory-acceptance but also the archived-old retrieval process itself, which gathers the archived-old **fodder** responsible for provisioning the vast combinations and permutations.

In other words, the direct consequence of differing sensory-acceptance and data-archive retrieval is that significances between people will vary from trivial to momentous.

Additionally and of prime importance for discussions of new pro-habit creation are that Habit-Patterns will also correspondingly vary.

This is great news because Devise-Mulling is thereby enabled to create something new by choice.

As we will continue to uncover, Devise-Mulling accomplishes individual uniqueness by not only varying Bombardment-Sphere influences via its **Test-IT**s but also purposeful data-archive and 'Puzzle' creation and Solutioning.

Habit-Patterns

Therefore, although one's teeth brushing Habit-Pattern seems normal to you, observation will quickly reveal others brush their teeth slightly-to-radically differently.

Here are a few posers. First, why are so many Habitual variances possible between members of our species: and what mechanisms are at work that enable these variances?

Secondly, how are Habit-Patterns created and maintained through decades: and furthermore how does a Habit-Pattern just transparently deploy 'mindlessly' or without requiring aware contribution?

Thirdly, how are so many differences possible between peoples Habit-Patterns?

Fourth and of paramount importance though, how many Habit-Patterns are persistently functioning without your awareness and driving your second-by-second, daily, yearly and lifetime existence in less than useful directions?

> Most vitally, how many Habit-Patterns are obstructing you from fulfilling or even knowing your passions?

Additionally, which of those Habit-Patterns are harmful addictions and/or destructive behaviors.

Create Your Own Pro-Habits

Would it not be great to understand how these automated Habit-Pattern powerhouses operate?

Without doubt, it would be enormously beneficial as one could then consciously intercede to create their very own new and super-beneficial Habit-Patterns.

In other words, would it not be awesome to know how to create Habit-Patterns that would strive, automatically and effortlessly in the background (as this is their inherent nature) to get you what you **TRULY** want?

The good news is **Habit-Patterns** do exist. The better news is that once you know **How-We-Work**, i.e., what drives these second-by-second Habit-Pattern actioners, you are truly enabled to intervene and supersede malfunctioning detrimental Habit-Patterns by exercising conscious choice to create new pro-habits.

How Habits Work

As Habits initiate the vast majority of one's 'normal' day-to-day actions, it is obvious that Habits are critical to understand.

However, before plunging into discussions regarding how to create more useful habits, one must first understand their multi-purposes: how they work, what triggers them, and so forth.

> First, keep in mind there are two types of Habits, not just one: Forming the **Habit-Duo** are Body-Habits (or Soma-Habits) and Mind-Habits (or Cognitive-Habits).

Although both Habit-Duo members were discussed in the first two books, a restatement of their characteristics in terms of **Tactics** will be valuable at this point.

> Also though, feel free to utilize the indexes in the first two books in order to review sections regarding Habit-Duo, Self-Duo, Soma-Habits, Cognitive-Habits, etc.

When Soma-sensors are being inundated by recognized and low intensity event Deluge, Soma-Habits are responsible for rapid responder **Soma-Actions**.

> Please peruse the Soma-Self graphic at IS-102 in the last section of this book.

Well before Soma-Action is initiated however, a sensory-accepted event has transitioned from a Deluge events 'impact' mechanical energy into a specific frequency **action-potential.**

An **a**ction-potential signature is uniquely based on several circumstances: the Soma-event impact type (smell; touch; taste; sound; etc.: not sight); the event intensity; plus the impact Location-ID (body or soma area receiving the sensory-acceptance).

> The stability of the Soma-Self created action-potential is critical because action-potential is the **neural-currency** standard that gets utilized by all following assessment processors: whether by Soma-Self and/or in definable circumstances by Cognitive-Self as well.

In Soma-sensor Deluge situations large numbers of soma-neurons fire, possibly across a broad scope of **Location-IDs**: This resultantly causes a dramatic spike in neural activity.

Consequently, the quantity of activated neurons within each Location-ID equates to its event-horizon neuron activity-gradient and therefore to event intensity.

Survival

Notably, frequency clues, accepted by sensory-apparatus for decades have been utilized to populate data-archives.

Therefore, it is simplest to think of Habit-Patterns as pre-assessed risk managers. This is so because Habit-Patterns have been formulated to keep one safe. They consistently and predictably accomplish this by utilizing populated data-archive frequency repositories or information storehouses for comparative-analysis.

Undeniably, as action-potentials have been gathered and then storehoused in tens-of-thousands of frequency dedicated neural mass since birth, data-archives exist as the underpinning for comparative-analysis (i.e., current-new to archived-old assessment).

Restated then, the specific purpose of data-archive action-potential accumulation is to form frequency based data-repositories so applicable processors can use them to compare the current event stream in order to first determine recognition-status (recognized or not) and then second, after integration with equivalent archived-old frequencies, select the best-to-date rapid Habitual response.

In other words, once recognition and intensity are determined, physical movement toward superior Bombardment-Sphere conditions is the next order of business. This is accomplished by deploying either/or Habitual Soma-Self and Cognitive-Self response-patterns.

Cognitive-Self response-patterns accumulated from years of specific frequency group sensory-accepted archived data are melded into Test-It's.

Learning how to ride a bike will be used as an example of Habit-Pattern creation and deployment.

As there are thousands and thousands of sensory combinations of various complexities necessary to accomplish bike riding, the example will be dramatically simplified. It will instead assume that there are only five modest requirements: getting the bike upright; straddling the bike; holding the handlebars; peddling; and balancing.

As explained above, recognition and intensity are keys to Soma-Self and Cognitive-Self engagement.

Therefore, it is important to note at the outset of learning how to ride that everything will be not only UN-recognized (i.e., minimal data-archives) but also of high intensity (i.e., one will feel apprehensive because of the unknown, which is equivalent to minimal archived-old data).

Even though the explanations below make little attempt to discriminate between Soma-Self and Cognitive-Self duties, both are involved. Remember, in any situation where either UN-recognized and/or higher intensity exists, Soma-Self will create a **Cognitive-Alert** purposed to additionally engage Cognitive-Self to **Figure-It-Out** and find **The-Ways**.

You are determined to master this skill and become proficient: it is what you TRULY and passionately want.

The first task of 'getting the bike upright' goes smoothly. Although the action feels weird (because comparative Experience-Senses are minimal) at first (i.e., the process is UN-recognized and high-intensity).

This sensation soon dissipates however as the newness of the current event-stream quickly becomes Soma-Self recognized due to the rapid population of frequency appropriate data-archives.

Furthermore, the task ultimately gets handled by Soma-Self: i.e., without the need for further alerts to Cognitive-Self.

This is because Soma-Actions are initiated by Soma-Habits due to the event-stream becoming recognized with corresponding reduced intensity. Thus, Cognitive-Self apprehension also dissolves due to the cessation of Cognitive-Alerts (i.e., the task now seems a no-brainer: which is actually true as no Cognitive-Alerts are being received).

Only a small number of sensory events (in our simplified example) are necessary to fulfill this first step.

Competency with this task and the comfort (Experience-Sense) that comes with it is due to appropriate Soma-Self and Cognitive-Self frequency data-archives quickly reaching **evaluative-sufficiency**: i.e., recognized comparative evaluation of current-new to archived-old.

Feeling accomplished (Experience-Sense) at having created a new-habit set regarding the mission of getting the bike upright, you are ready for the next task: straddling or throwing your leg over the bikes upper bar.

Each stages sequence of attempting and practicing remains relatively the same.

In other words, that which is at first **UN**-recognized and higher-intensity to Soma-Self, which resultantly calls on Cognitive-Self for assistance via Soma-Self created Cognitive-Alerts, gradually becomes recognized and low-intensity.

Simultaneously, Mind-Self has processed received Cognitive-Alerts and consequently brought its Cognitive-Sensors or vision to bear.

Once busy creating and sending action suggestions or Test-Its of various complexities that also gather feedback to Solution Puzzles, Cognitive-Self (or Mind-Self) is now peaceful. It has dutifully fulfilled its assistant mandate of Figuring-It-Out and finding The-Ways.

Soma-Self (or Body-Self) data-archives are not the only ones to benefit. Cognitive-Self also created data-archives including Cognitive-Habits, which will also be utilized for all future comparative-analysis.

In other words, next time similar frequencies (current-new) are presented like when riding a different bike, Cognitive responses will be much more rapid because its significantly-similar (archived-old) matching capability provides a huge leg up in creating more honed to current-event Test-Its.

Thus, there is truth in the saying that 'everything is **hard** until it becomes **easy**'.

As How-We-Work is now better understood, the above statement can be reiterated in *Way Better* Your L.I.F.E^2. terms.

Everything **UN**-recognized and higher intensity is **hard** due to insufficient population of Body-Self and Mind-Self data-archives.

In other words, a current data-stream remains **UN**-recognized **until comparative analysis** of current-new to archived-old deems the event as recognized, which of course is due to sufficient data-archive population because of sensory-acceptance, which is in turn due to **DO**ing.

At this point the task becomes **easy** and minimally stressful (Experience-Sense) due to the rapid deployment of created Soma-Self and Cognitive-Self Habit-Patterns.

Comparative Analysis

The above being said, the existence of data-archiving capability tenders a fundamental and intriguing question: Why are sensory-accepted morphed frequencies stored in the first place?

No question genetics has provided humans huge neural capacity for both processing and storage. How did this come about?

Was neural capacity adaptively spawned because our species essentially taunts 'problematic' by being physically designed to move vigorously about in their Bombardment-Spheres?

In other words, was genetics inspired to reach into and engage more of its potential dormant range as an adaptive response to the increased sensory-input due to greater mobility, which thereby induces extreme survival conditions, thus prompting the need for granular 'recognition'?

OR

Was it perhaps the spontaneous arrival of neural resources that by provisioning extreme capacity (and therefore adaptability) taunts potentially damaging Bombardment-Sphere events by spiriting our nearly fanatical seeking of the unfamiliar?

Regardless of causality, because of human desire to seek and move, survival became much more challenging. Fortunately, genetics provided two universe synchronous integrated methodologies to accommodate our danger laced seeking compulsion: comparative analysis and the Habit-Duo.

> Intriguingly, both capabilities are not only fundamental to survival but also utilize the same core universe feature for both storage (data-archiving) and retrieval (recall): Frequency stability.

Without doubt effective comparative analysis first hinges on the comparator (sensory-accepted event) and comparatee (data-archive or stored action-potential) having synchronous frequency.

Remember from books one and two, that two principles regarding unwavering symmetry are important as we rely upon them for our existence.

> A Matched-Base-Frequency Bracket tenaciously sustains its action-potential frequency for decades (the comparatee): and the universe unchangeably provides all the reliable frequencies (comparators) with which we are being bombarded. Notably recall would be difficult or impossible, if either were in flux.

Secondly, neural-processors must be able to search data-resources by common frequency (comparator to comparatee) to determine if a **same** (in the case of Soma-Self) or **significantly-similar** (in the case of Cognitive-Self) comparatee exists: or not.

Only one of two possibilities can be delivered by a frequency retrieval search: either a located 'event' is **recognized** or if not located, the 'event' is **UN**-recognized.

Regardless, comparative analysis by Soma-Self and Cognitive-Self is definitely a mainstay of human survival. Intriguingly, deployment of this strategy is elegant by nature of its simplicity.

> Comparative analysis then, in order to perform 'recognition' of current-events is specifically purposed (for both Soma-Self and Cognitive-Self) to implement **frequency-comparison** of a **current-new** sensory-accepted Deluge event to an **archived-old** frequency synchronous stored data-element.

Recognition capability or event-recognition is critical as it not only saves 'reinventing the wheel' each time a same-frequency is encountered (potentially hundreds of times a second) but also enables a faster patterned response and thus much greater survival-potential.

So, whether instigated directly by Body-Self Soma-actions or Mind-Self action requests (Test-Its), responding is a much more complex process than 'simple' accessing of warehoused Matched-Base-Frequency SLID and VLID (Soma-Location-ID and Visual-Location-ID) action-potentials.

For these advanced responding processes to be effective, more complex broader-scope frequency-harmonics (as discussed in books one and two) are necessary.

> To cut to the chase though, whereas one's data-archive neural arrays are all about action-potential **frequency-storing** of one kind or another (whether as base-frequencies or blended-harmonics), neural-processor arrays are all about **frequency-recall** and frequency recognition and evaluation of current-data (current-new) to retrieved archived-old data.

Fortuitously for broader-scope possibilities, not all neural-arrays are created equal. Soma-Self provisions neural-pathways with only a few connections between Matched-Base-Frequency data-archives, whereas Cognitive-Self provisions hundreds and even thousands of interconnected pathways into alternate frequency data-archive realms.

> Significantly, for 'higher' cognitive functioning to be effective, large quantities of connections enable much more dynamic frequency data-comparisons.

In fact, Soma-Self comparisons only deal with '**same**' current-new to archived-old. Any other condition but 'same' is determined **problematic**.

Such assessment results in packaging the 'problematic' current-new data-event and then sending it outbound via Cognitive-Alert to its more robust Cognitive-Self companion for evaluation, feedback and cyclical 'Solutioning' suggestions via Test-Its.

Significantly-Similar

Wonderfully, Mind-Self provisions a **game-changing** processing leap.

This is due to its capability to expansively manage a gradient of comparatives from SAME through **significantly-similar**. This capacity also thereby empowers proactive extrapolation or expansive thinking, problem solving and invention.

Incredibly, significantly-similar processing is radically different than the way Universe-H works. Recall Universe-H is steadfast in its presentation of SAME (Electromagnetic Frequency Spectrum) right from its fundamental energy building blocks, which through different mixtures presents the elementary particle 'mass' building-blocks of matter: the proton, neutron and electron.

It is through the energy building-blocks remaining SAME that matter signatures (frequencies) remain absolutely constant or permanently SAME.

In other words, once an atomic particle is formed, it is ostensibly immutable: except perhaps in the core of a massive star, where heat and pressure are unfathomable.

Stated differently, tin remains tin and gold remains gold etc. because of Universe-H providing immutable energy building-blocks. Without that fundamental in place our cosmos would be a broth of ever changing mush like a small muddy pond that has been stirred up.

Phenomenally, all the frequencies that sensory-arrays accept also work due to Universe-H's delivery of immutable SAME frequencies. Therefore, all data-archives are consistently populated with their particular SAME current-new as well.

So, in a universal view, Universe-H has provision of SAME down to a fine art. However, something I find most incredible, we humans provide something quite different: mixable significantly-similar.

I herein postulate data-archive variance to be of particular significance for the expansion or growth of Universe-H.

My following reasoning is further discussed in the "Attraction" section below.

Definite is that even though sensory-arrays function very similarly one person to the next and thus similarly gather Deluge, both sensory-acceptance and fodder recombination by Cognition-Complex and Devise-Mulling Puzzle creation and Solutioning processes are not SAME but different.

Thus, it is due to ongoing recombination of sensory-accepted action-potentials that get morphed into one's **neurological-currency** or fodder that significantly contributes (along with physical mass) to the subtle to large vibrational differences between people.

In other words, data-archive population variances actually cause each person to vibrate at a slightly different frequency.

Although one's vibrational frequency is within Universe-H's gradient-of-acceptability, none of these people-frequencies are directly produced by any of Universe-H's many SAME generating processes.

Therefore, we are each unique frequency generating sites that just like each instrument in an orchestra, which provide their unique part of the whole generated **sound-harmonic**, likewise provide our frequencies into the pool of frequencies needed to enrich our frequency-based Universe-H.

Let me state this in a different, perhaps more user-friendly way. Universe-H, through its consistent Laws-of-Frequency provides the seven basic music notes from A to G.

> If one cuts, affixes and tightens a length of 'string', it will always (in same conditions) yield the same frequency. All stringed musical instruments rely on the immutability of string length (and other characteristics) to produce the same noise: in other words, SAME.

However, along comes Mind-Self's Puzzle creating and Devise-Mulling's Solutioning complexes. They not only sensory-accept these seven immutable frequencies but also do something quite remarkable. They instigate significantly-similar.

Not only are the basic seven notes sliced and diced into other Universe-H acceptable frequencies but they are attenuated, morphed and changed by the introduction of harmonic combinations, different instruments, strength and duration of note play and values, etc. Without significantly-similar the same note played on a piano would be wholly different than if played on a Saxophone, than on a guitar, etc.

Universe-H reiterates whereas Homo sapiens extrapolate.

Significantly-similar then is one of the major Keys to *Way Better* Your L.I.F.E^2.

As such, its ramifications will continue to be discussed. Point is that discovery driven by significantly-similar revelations is excellent for enhancing living-experiences, whereas limiting assumptions about what is possible for you based on outdated domesticated self-doubt chaos-habits such as, addictions, self-destructive desires, etc. is not.

> Broader evaluation scope however has a cost: processing duration. Specifically, Body-Self having few choices or pathway options can respond hundreds of times faster than Mind-Self.

On the flip side, Cognitive-Self by providing more vast and complex neural-pathways and data-archives greatly expands Soma-Self's limited 'stimulus-response' survival mandate.

Thereby, Cognitive-Self competencies additionally enable all we value as people: awareness; volition; choice; ingenuity and the cognitive features list go on and on.

> Clearly, the Soma-Self and Cognitive-Self mechanisms responsible for **How-We-Work** were also gifted by genetics.

The **Self-Duo** diagram, employed in *Way Better* Your L.I.F.E^2.: Body-Self or *Way Better* Your L.I.F.E^2.: Mind-Self and additionally provided in this books illustration section at IS-101, graphically encompass all mechanisms, which determine **How-We-Work** from sensory-acceptance origins through to behaviours, cognition, personality, et al.

Remarkably, slight variances in human DNA (deoxyribonucleic acid), genomes or genetic-templates determine 'people-differences' in foundational capability and capacity.

As each genome varies, so does DNAs vibrational-harmonic, whose reliable variances are easily discernable for each biological entity.

Thus, all humans vibrate slightly differently one from the next within the very small range that defines us.

Variances may very well account for the immediate 'sense' (Experience-Sense) one has of those with whom one comes in contact.

In other words, the more similarly one vibrates in relation to another the more in harmony one feels with them: whereas great vibrational differences can make a 'cold chill go up your spine'.

Stated more granularly, differences among people then partly arise due to slightly different configurations of a few of the three billion plus unbelievably small 'base-pair' DNA molecular components.

Harmoniously to the universe standard, human DNA's twenty-three chromosome paired groups present a holistic frequency vibration as well.

Additionally though, as is the standard, each chromosome also individually spawns a particular vibrational harmonic.

The Master Enabler

Now clear is that frequency is the enabler for all How-We-Work mechanisms and methodologies, which are responsible for driving not only sensory acquisition, neurophysiological transitional functionality and data-storage but also recall, cognition and Habitual responses.

Critically then, the first two books disclosed frequency as the backbone to How-We-Work.

In other words, the first two books detailed strategies ranging from neural-facilities responsible for Soma-Actions to Cognitive-Self **Solutioning** and awareness through to portrayal of one's reality by the **Movie-of-Your-Life** presentation center.

Way Better Your L.I.F.E^2.: Tactics takes a different approach than either *Way Better* Your L.I.F.E^2.: Body-Self or *Way Better* Your L.I.F.E^2.: Mind-Self as it discloses methodologies to apply the **How-We-Work** principles provided in books one and two to enhance significantly one's day-to-day living-adventures or **L.I.F.E².**: this author's acronym for Living-in-Full-Experience-and-Excitement.

However, as the first two books clarified how both Body-Self and Mind-Self work they will be utilized as reference works for this third book of the series.

Book-Three, '**Tactics**' details strategies to Create-Your-Habits (new more useful ones) and stop allowing Your-Habits-Create-You (the limiting domesticated ones).

Tactics will disclose how to not only actively engage Self-Duo to mine Habit-Power's massive renewable resource but also exploit Cognition-Complex to better Figure-It-Out and find The-Ways.

More succinctly stated, *Way Better* Your L.I.F.E².: Tactics is purposed to explain critical strategies that will positively integrate **How-We-Work** knowledge into one's daily living-experience and thus enhance experiences and excitement.

Among other pertinent issues, discussions will encompass how to not only effectively engage and deploy Self-Duo mechanisms at will to create pro-habits that will continuously work to get you what you want but also easily turn-on and sustain conscious awareness for extended periods thereby releasing one's massive potential.

In other words, to ensure both the **Habit-Force** and the **Choosing-Force** be with you (couldn't resist), **Tactics** will explain the concepts and methodologies necessary to purposefully, selectively and beneficially engage one's Self-Duo mechanisms (i.e., Body-Self and Mind-Self).

> The subtitle, **Are You Creating Habits to Get What You TRULY Want**, suggests how **Habit-Power** can be your automatic and continuously vigilant friend, entirely focused on fulfilling your wishes, your dreams: once you fully understand how they function of course.

Possibilities

How many potential evaluations are there for a short string of sensory-accepted Deluge events: such as experiencing sunset?

For instance, if it was possible to place a thousand adults in the sunset Deluge event stream, would perceptions and behaviour be identical for everyone? It is evident from previous discussions they would not: as no doubt there would be as many different perceptions (slight to considerable: some bored; some enthralled) as the number of folks watching this daily event.

> Differences would result because **current-new** is always integrated with **archived-old** (including the tempering effects of Tier-5 Experience-Senses) in order to regulate both Soma-responses and Cognitive-responses.

As archived-old will always vary between people as do fingerprints, so too will behavioural responses vary: Thus blossoms each person's uniqueness.

As so many valuation possibilities exist for ongoing Deluge, what mechanisms are actually operating to provide both rapid response and individual consistency?
Of course, the answer here is Habit-Patterns. To maintain critical individualized uniformity Habit-Patterns provide the core strategy, which always spawns from comparison and assessment of archived-old (memory if you like) to current-new.

> This incredible comparative capability is powerful because Habit-Patterns thus not only enable individualized responses but also provide predictable response sets, which additionally promote best global outcome (survival) not only for the one but often for the group as well.

If Habit-Patterns were not active, predictability and survival would be out the window. This is because each situation would always seem new: even if truly being repeated.

Thus, would not only **Solutioning** require massive brain-mass resources, which are simply not available but also responses be too slow to be Survival useful: i.e., they would not be capable of auto-responding you to safety.

Therefore, once the mechanisms, which determine **How-We-Work** are understood, you will be on the path to creating your own pro-habits, which will enable you to easily Live-In-Full-Experience-and-Excitement.

The best news is that once a Habit-Pattern set is recognized as not useful, new and more powerful Habit-Pattern drivers can be **choice-created** by deploying Habit-Power.

Additionally, choice-created new pro-habits can be totally focussed on getting you what you TRULY want while simultaneously usurping old chaos-habits, which are interfering with actualizing your hopes, wishes and dreams.

What Drives You

If you have ever pondered such things as: what drives you to do what you do; what are the origins or essence of your understandings, perceptions and behaviours; what is responsible for slight to great differences between family members and people; or why we exist, you are reading the right book.

In fact, the Force-of-Habit series are the only volumes (as of the publishing date), which comprehensively address and answer these and many related questions.

For instance and without resorting to pedantic, religious or unsubstantiated references, *Way Better* Your L.I.F.E². clearly explains the age-old questions of not only why we exist in this universe but also our purpose.

> *Way Better* Your L.I.F.E². takes great care to build its cases. It bases rationales on various definable premises, which once integrated by explanation provide self-evident truths as to **How-We-Work**.

One might rightly ask why build such a comprehensive compendium to explain How-We-Work?

> The answer is straightforward. Once one knows how they or anything truly works, it opens a panorama of user possibilities.

Once you know how you truly work, this powerful knowledge can be utilized to make choices that are substantially more effective: Not just the 'big' conscious ones but also more importantly all those second-by-second habit driven ones, which actually run one's living-experience.

Self-Duo's Soma-Habits and Cognitive-Habits (SHABs and CHABs) are so powerful because they work continuously, consistently and predictably 24/7 running most of one's day.

Does it not then make sense that both the creation and deployment methodologies of these silent and diligent workhorses be understood fully?

It is evident that only once one understands how something works, whether a simple fork or more complex human neural-physiological mechanisms can its features be utilized for maximum benefit.

Thereby, only by understanding how Soma-Habits and Cognitive-Habits come to power one's day, can one hope to create specific pro-habits, which will work automatically and continuously to get you what you TRULY want: And, when wisely orchestrated, positively enhance ones living experience.

Whether aware of habitual dictates or not, probably 'not' as this is their 'silent' or transparent nature, everyone relies on the consistent outcomes of both Soma-Habits and Cognitive-Habits.

For instance, it would not do to have to concentrate on each step you take or refigure out the mechanics of how to hold a pen or type, etc.

> Recall that Cognitive-Habits come to epitomize beliefs, expectations, assumptions and so much more.

Experience-Senses of course derive from ongoing sensory-accepted Deluge events in the first place, which are utilized to create Tier-One through Tier-Five data-archives.

Significantly, as current-data is processed through Cognitive–Pathways, it is 'swayed' or adjusted to conform to recalled frequency-triggered Experience-Senses, thus biasing one's current perceptions in relation to previous experiences.

> For example, 'new' is easier for young children because they have not had the exposure (sensory-acceptance) to create large action-potential Experience-Senses that limit and thus interfere with current-new sensory-acceptance.

Predictability and tenaciously, sameness are the hallmarks of both types of habits: Soma-Self for the body or physical portion of habitual patterned reactions and Cognitive-Self for the more intricate Cognitive-Cluster response servings.

Tactics:

Deeper

Prom birth and probably even a few months before, one continually navigates their Bombardment-Sphere or surrounding environment, either habitually or with some degree of awareness, to either avoid obstacles and/or improve conditions.

Reliably, obstacles and Bombardment-Sphere conditions, whether real or concocted, like everything else in the universe, present within a range or gradient from inconsequential to vital.

In other words, obstacles can vary from innocuous, like a closed door, to survival critical, like avoiding a car rapidly bearing down on your position. Comparatively, contrived conditions also present within broad ranges: such as from mild apprehension to immobilizing fear of the unfamiliar.

Regardless however, as all current-new and archived-old information originated as sensory-accepted Bombardment, its resulting action-potential neural-currency is what is utilized to enable **navigation**.

Beliefs and thoughts do not exist independent
of sensory-accepted Bombardment:
Indeed all the meanings one creates are formed from it.

In fact, sensory-accepted Bombardment is the source or **fodder** for everything one is and one can become: Therefore, the value of **sensory-origins** cannot be over emphasized.

Incredibly, as will become clear in this book, the origin of sensory-acceptance holds an **essential key** to enhancing one's living-experience.

Enabling the myriad of capabilities necessary for successful 'navigation' is genetics. Besides the obvious biological forum, it gifts five substantial key-resources to maximize survival potential and/or enhance living conditions.

Most importantly though, the main thrust of *Way Better* Your L.I.F.E^2.: **Tactics** narrative is to explain 'how-to' maximize living conditions.

During following discussions, please utilize *Way Better* Your L.I.F.E^2.: Body-Self or *Way Better* Your L.I.F.E^2.: Mind-Self indexes to reference explanation(s) when any presented expression or concept is unfamiliar or unclear.

Foddering

On the front line of all one is, are sensory-detectors. Two independent yet fully interactive sensor-types are available 24/7 to identify what is going on **Out-There**: Soma-sensors and Cognitive-sensors.

Soma-sensors provide various arrays of physical or Soma (body) event-horizon workhorses, which actively gather different types of impact information from the Deluge.

Assisting Soma sensor-arrays are Cognitive-sensors (visual). Their miraculous configuration provides not only supportive feedback for Soma-sensors via Cognitive-Alerts but also independent **remarkable-feature** detection. Additionally, survival-critical proactive evaluations are accomplished as well when Cognitive-sensors interact with powerful cognitive processors.

Secondly, genetics has provided a means to store or archive sensory information for the sole purpose of recognition-analysis. In this way, one can move through their ever-morphing Bombardment-Sphere recognizing innocuous events that do not require special attention and focus on **UN**-recognized and/or high-intensity, potentially survival critical happenings, which do.

> This **exception-strategy** enhances survival potential by not only maximizing response-capacity for **current-new** but also effectively and efficiently utilizing limited neural-resources: thus not wasting them on mundane or non-threatening occurrences.

Thirdly, repetitively recognized events inspire sensory specific response-patterns. Storehoused in specialized neural-archives these incredible actioners, Soma-Habits and Cognitive-Habits, keep us safe and on track.

As indicated above there are two types of Habits (the Habit-Duo). Namely, Soma-Habits, which deal with physical responses; and more complex multi-tier Cognitive-Habits, which deal with perceptions, beliefs, assumptions, etc.

Fourthly, genetics has provided an array of processors, which not only cross-compare current-new to archived-old but evaluate event intensity.

> Such evaluations are critical if response to the 'current-event / archived-data retrieval package' is to be occurrence proportionate.

Fifthly, provision has been made to enable Cognitive-Self to send an array intensity specific **action-packets** called Test-Its to Soma-Self to both adjust physical position within one's Bombardment-Sphere and gather additional sensory feedback (due to new positioning) until the **current-new** or **problematic** crisis is normalized.

One might well ask at this juncture: How is such incredibly intricate handling from sensory-acceptance to archiving, to cross-comparison, to appropriate response, to Test-Its, to the creation of attitudes et al, proportionately and accurately managed? What is the underlying commonality?

The first two books exposed and detailed **How-We-Truly-Work** as an interactive habitual and cognitive species.

They utilized the unique Self-Duo model to underline not only one's survival critical Soma-Self and Cognitive-Self Force-of-Habit mandates but also how, little by little you become you as a consequence of neural-manipulation by genetically engineered mechanisms of sensory-accepted fragments from one's Bombardment-Sphere.

Now detailed foundations have been laid, *Way Better* Your L.I.F.E². : Tactics takes a different tack. It expands upon the detailed processes to explain **so-what**.

> In other words, now we know How-We-Work, *Way Better* Your L.I.F.E². : Tactics explains how this knowledge can be applied to improve one's living-experience.

However, for discussions about **Tactics** to apply in all situations, they must integrate the common aspect upon which not only every characteristic of Universe-H but also one's 'reality' or Movie-Of-Your-Life is founded.

To say the least, uncovering the essence of everything seemed formidable.

Frequency

However, the first two Force-of-Habit books did accomplish the seemingly impossible by disclosing frequency as the crux, center-point or underpinning of every aspect of both our universe and our functioning.

> Unquestionably then, in **Universe-H** (coined in *Way Better* Your L.I.F.E².: **Body**), if it doesn't vibrate; it doesn't exist.

This statement is certain because energy as well as all its various atomic amalgamations as 'matter' exhibit consistent, stable and immutable vibrational frequencies without which identifiability of anything would be impossible.

> Consequently, predictably and fortuitously, hydrogen remains hydrogen, photons persist as photons, rainbows always present colors (frequencies) in the same order, gold stays gold, water is water and so on.

Broader Application

In much broader application however, frequencies are the touch-point or essential factor for not only non-corporeal existence (that which one would not consider alive) but also corporeal animation as well.

> In other words, whether matter assembles to support corporeal drive or instead endures to provide the vast repositories of non-corporeal 'soup' enabling animation, frequency is the underpinning for Universe-H existence.

In order to delineate the pervasiveness of Universe-H frequency stability, dedicated research has categorized both the parameters and juxtapositions of known and theorized vibrational-frequencies.

To catalogue the enormous magnitude of frequency-members, a linear frequency scale called the Electromagnetic Spectrum or more descriptively, the Electromagnetic Frequency Spectrum was devised. It establishes an extremely useful Universe-H frequency register.

> Simply stated, it provisions an immutable vibrational frequency 'spot' on its very long gradient or linear-scale for all the energy and matter stuff in Universe-H.

The Electromagnetic Spectrum register is extensive: from the smallest energy remnant; to energies many atomic matter expressions; to molecular compounds formed of atomic building-block 'material'; to vast arrays of cooperatively interacting molecular compounds (some, like DNA, which enable life forms); right up to the universe itself.

> Resultantly, the third book in the *Way Better* Your L.I.F.E[2]. series, *Way Better* Your L.I.F.E[2].: **Tactics**, expands upon the building-block role frequency plays to explain 'higher' functions: like Soma and Cognitive habits, thinking, behaviour, personality, etc.

Before leaping to cognitive function explanations though, it is first vital to understand the concert that frequencies enable within one's biological systems.

Frequency Stability

Understanding of frequency-stability is crucial because a grasp of the critical building-block nature of frequencies is core to appreciating not only the "simple-complexity" of How-We-Work but also the efficacy of how one both blends with the non-corporeal Out-There and coexists in harmony with the Universe-H dynamic mosaic.

> Crucially, frequency stability is not only the very core of existence ensuring energy and its atomic building block derivatives remain immutable and discrete but also the reason the myriads of energy derived atomic components cooperatively and consistently interact without losing individual identities.

Incredibly, frequency stability ensures the integrity of atomic particle vibrational signatures when either independent as in the case of 'elements' or assembled into larger molecular compound amalgams.

In other words, frequencies tenacious non-mixing strategy enables the co-existence of atoms without **mushing** when in larger 'matter' constructs: these auspiciously present their own vibrational group-frequency as well.

> Frequency autonomy is critical to existence, as we know it, because if 'mushing' of energy and/or particle frequencies were possible, our Universe-H cosmos would have become a lifeless homogeneous undefinable blend a long time ago.

Sensory-Apparatus

Also incredibly, energies frequency-discrete feature has direct Tactics to why both biological (body or soma) and neuro-physiological (nervous, cerebral and cognitive) systems predictably work.

Due to the vast range of frequencies on the Electromagnetic Frequency Spectrum, it would definitely be hugely problematic if humans had sensory-receptors for every possible Universe-H frequency because both processing and storage requirements would be untenable.

Opportunely, the mechanics of sensory-apparatus mechanisms are inherently frequency limiting. This means each sensory-neuron accepts only its own small sliver of frequency events.

For instance, although many examples are available, their rigorous censorship is why ears don't see and eyes don't hear.

Tolerable-Signal

> Phenomenally, the **living-process** (all we have come to know and become) is initialized by diverse arrays of bio-mechanical sensory-system neurological-acceptors or event-horizon managers, which are in play to 'pick-up' or 'data-capture' from the Deluge their specific limited frequency-range or Tolerable-Signal.

Additionally policing potential Deluge inundation and overload, sensory-system marvels do not uptake all Bombardment within their frequency-range either but instead mechanically determine acceptability by utilizing two very effective biomechanical regulating strategies.

Threshold-Potential

First, to sensory-accept, a neuron must be in a **ready-state**; not in **refresh-mode**. Second, to activate a 'ready-state' sensor-neuron, the Bombardment-event must present with sufficient intensity, force or Threshold-Potential.

> In other words, a sensory-receptor neuron when in 'ready-state' only accepts a Tolerable-Signal Deluge-event with sufficient Threshold-Potential or intensity: Otherwise, it is ignored or filtered out.

Conclusively, disparate sensory-systems due to genetically tailored specializations are extremely proficient biological frequency and intensity filters. Their structures thus provide an interface, which form 'Level-one' of a host of survival methodologies.

> Almost inconceivably, while front-line sensory-system event-horizons endure massive and unrelenting energy and particle Deluge 24/7, steadfast biological filtering receptor neurons are busily weeding out most noxious Bombardment.

Species Viability

Extraordinarily, human species viability is actually 100% enabled by sensory-apparatus capabilities: albeit only within a substantially narrowed frequency **range-of-acceptance**.

Stated differently, the restricted 'range-of-acceptance' as deployed by sensory-systems, limits, biologically rejects or filters-out most of the massive Deluge at an event-horizon, thus facilitating survival.

> Based on current human accomplishments, the sensory-receptor 'bio-filtering' or **frequency-compromise** strategy has certainly proved more beneficial than a hindrance: at least to date.

I say 'at least to date' because, if humans continue inexcusable erosion of the fragile environment and thus its marvelous physical-world filters, which keep us safe by maintaining a livable Bombardment-Sphere, then one's sensory-apparatus will be correspondingly compromised.

If this occurs, as sensory contribution is everything one is and can become, resultant sensory degradation will negatively affect one's capability to not only understand but also design a serviceable and survivable reality.

Frequency Handling

Now foundations have been discussed, it is exciting to note sensory-acceptance is just the beginning of an incredible process, which ultimately enables the formation and presentation of one's reality.

To manage the Deluge, one is genetically equipped with four diverse, interactive **frequency-handling** stages: namely, capture (sensory-systems); transmit (neural-channels); process (evaluative-processors); and store (data-archiving).

Capture

Priming the frequency-handling event progression is 'capture' or sensory-acceptance, which was introduced above. Even at this earliest stage though, 'frequency-handling' is substantially more dynamic than just first 'sensory-accepting' and then indifferently shuffling 'raw-data' along to the next 'neural-venue'.

This is because, although all sensory-systems first morph a sensory-accepted Deluge 'raw-data' event into an action-potential or **signal**, each additionally integrates specific **acceptance-site** or frequency location identification information into its subsequent signal **transmission** to a follow-on stage.

Such acceptance-site **signal-augmenting**, depending on whether the acceptance originated with Body-Self Soma-Sensors or Mind-Self Cognitive-Sensors is designed to frequency-transform an originating Deluge events mechanical energy signal into a tailored **SLID** or **VLID** 'action-potential' **Tag** (Soma-Location **ID**entifier and Visual-Location **ID**entifier, respectively).

Transmit

Once 'capture' and signal morphing is accomplished, a SLID or VLID **Tag** (action-potential) is transmitted via common neural pathways. This is incredible because, although common neural-channels are utilized, 'Tags' originating at different acceptance sites do not blend or homogeneously mix but remain absolutely discrete.

> Distinctness is achievable due to an immutable frequency characteristic **Key** of Universe-H discussed earlier called **Signal-Persistence**, which assures disparate Tag signals or frequencies do not mix but remain discrete throughout the neural-processing regimen.

Signal-Persistence is easily observable by looking into the clear night sky. Even though the tens-of-thousands of visible stars created identical photons (light) and even though their photons traversed trillions of trillions of miles over billions and billions of years through inconceivable energy and particle events, their 'signals' have not mushed together. Thereby, one is able to view each discretely.

> Therefore, as if to ratify everything in Universe-H is in synchronous harmony, the fortitude of Signal-Persistence provides major benefit to corporeal animation as well as to non-corporeal existence.

In other words, due also to Signal-Persistence, a morphed 'action-potential' (the distinct SLID or VLID Tag) is also discretely transmitted via common neural channels without 'mushing' together.

> This frequency feature thus ensures the data-integrity of both Bombardment-event and its impact event-horizon location to applicable 'follow-on' mechanisms.

Resultantly, you are able to recall both the location and intensity of a touch because this information was provided by signal-augmenting at the event-horizon.

Process

Second-stage signal 'transmission' accomplishes arrival at the first mechanism. Here all individual frequency equivalent 'Tags' (i.e., those from the same location) are assembled into homogeneous **Tag-Cluster** groups.

However, Tag-Cluster action-potentials, as a consequence of 'Tag' amalgamation (many 'same' individual tags being grouped), are proportionately larger. Thereby, Tag-Clusters are utilized to determine **event-intensity** (how hard the touch was).

Critically, post amalgamation, Tag-Clusters become the 'element' that is utilized for evaluation, recalibration and/or comparative analysis (filtering) against archived-data.

Symmetrically, it is notable that archived-data was both stored and is subsequently retrievable (recalled) by utilizing the same frequency-standard as for everything else in Universe-H.

Storehouse or Archive

The last or storage-stage is accomplished by archiving-mechanisms, which are purposed to retain (slot) the finalized action-potentials into various referenceable 'frequency-compatible' data-archives, Brackets or Matched-Base-Frequency neural-arrays.

Critically, whether for Soma-Self or Cognitive-Self purposes, 'referenceable' neural 'real-estate' is comprised of assemblages of various quantities of neurons genetically predisposed to accept, as are the senses, only their specific frequency.

Such frequency-specific configuration serves survival requirements very well because recognition-processors are accordingly enabled to reliably fulfill not only 'current-data to stored-data' evaluation for recognition purposes but also perform **Devise-Mullings** broad-scope Cognitive-Self sentient functions.

Incredibly then, likewise do both data-archive 'Brackets' and neural-array processors invariably utilize the identical tried-and-true universe frequency principals to not only preserve (Filter-and-Slot) but also retrieve (recall) sensory-accepted data-elements or stored action-potential frequencies and/or more complex Harmonics.

Thus… due to Bracketing or data-archiving: little by little, you become you.

As both referenceable data-archives and ultimately Experience-Senses were derived as a consequence of certain aspects of the vibrational properties of energy and matter being first accepted by sensory-apparatus, then subsequently morphed, processed and stored, the critical role played by frequency cannot be overstated.

Universe-H vibrates; its components vibrate; we vibrate.

Harmoniously, we then utilize archived vibrational frequencies
to comprehend Universe-H.

We are in Sync.

Experientology

Conclusively then, everyone is interconnected with the fundamental frequency essence of Universe-H and thereby both synchronous and in vibrational harmony with it.

Let's examine how each person not only vibrates with his or her own unique frequency signature but also reciprocally **frequency-fodders** Universe-H.

Intriguingly, slight vibrational differences are scientifically measurable between people. In other words, a Human structure (Soma or body) vibrates within a particular narrow frequency range. Thus, as with everything else in Universe-H, humanity too has its position on the Electromagnetic Spectrum.

The reason for the slight vibrational variances between people is not only physical structure though but also sensory-accepted experiences accumulated in neural-repositories as action-potentials.

Specifically, two dynamic aspects are the sources of each person's overall differing vibrational composition. First, each person emanates a unique biological vibration due to slight genetic variances, one person to the next.

Secondly, distinctive personalized experiences storehoused within one's neural brain-mass as action-potentials, which remember also vibrate, additionally produce a unique combined vibration.

In other words, harmonic blending of these two vibrational sources (body and mind: Soma and Cognitive) actually produce a very specific and absolutely unique vibrational frequency for each and every person.

Understanding how physical structure can affect vibration is fairly straightforward because, and it may be obvious, vibration will slightly change due to more or less of the contributing materials (atoms, compounds, etc.).

> Notably, genetics plays a significant role in determining not only physical form but also Soma-Self and Cognitive-Self processing capabilities and data-archive capacities as well.

For instance, within the Human body each atom, molecule, compound and even a person's DNA (genetic material) consistently vibrates within its frequency range.
However, how might accumulated experiences have impact?
Recall Cognitive-Self experiences are maintained in Tier-One through Tier-Five data-archives.

Consequently, in that data-archives house action-potentials, which is energy that also uniquely vibrates within its frequency specific ranges, whose accumulation thus additionally impacts one's overall vibration.

Interestingly, as data-archives are populated over time, your baby-self will vibrate slightly differently than when an adult.

> Notably, those confident in their expert capabilities vibrate markedly differently than novices. Without pause, most can 'sense' this frequency variation almost instantly.

Stated differently, it is each person's special biological vibration, enacted by genetic variances, be they slight or pronounced, in concert with accumulated personalized experiences storehoused as action-potentials that provide millions of unique frequency signatures, which thereby reciprocally **frequency-fodder** Universe-H.

Therefore, in addition to the discrete vibrations of non-corporeal matter, not only does each person have a vital universe frequency-foddering purpose but so to do all members of each-and-every species of animal and plant as well as bacteria and archaea life forms.

Quite literally then, it is frequency, not 'matter', which animates each one of us. Conclusively, from sensory origins to data-archiving to recall … frequency is the binding cable.

> 'Matter' does not animate us because literally 99.9% plus of one's physical body-structure is non-corporeal: i.e., constructed of atoms and compounds without sentience.

Looking outbound at Universe-H, one is struck with the fact that it too, like the human body is mostly non-corporeal. However, it is not the preponderance of

Universe-H matter, but the potency of frequency, which I suggest is the determinant for sentience.

Therefore, by extrapolating from compelling similarities, I postulate that like us, Universe-H is thus also sentient.

> Additionally, does it not seem improbable that sentience could exist within a structure, which is not itself sentient?

In other words, could we be sentient if Universe-H was not? I postulate this as highly unlikely.

Thus the above revelation drives me to one additional conjecture as a consequence of the improbability statement above that "sentience could not exist within a structure, which is not itself sentient".

If that premise is so, then Universe-H, which is ipso facto a living system, must also exist within a structure, which is also a living system: let's call it Universe-A.

Furthermore, by following this line of reasoning Universe-A must also exist within a structure, which is also a living system, say Universe-B.

Such a postulate then accounts for infinite Universes not stacked side-by-side like book pages, as is the current scientific model but instead existing more like an onions structure: but with infinite sentient layers.

Such a layered structure could very well account for the 'birth' of our universe as well because like an onion, it too grows from the center, expanding ever outwards, as do its layers.

Tactics:

Broader-Scope

The Body-Self and Mind-Self sections immediately following are principally intended to support broader-scope **Tactics** discussions.

However, for those who have not yet had the opportunity to read *Way Better* Your L.I.F.E^2.: **Body-Self** or *Way Better* Your L.I.F.E^2.: **Mind-Self**, the ensuing detailed synopsis will provide excellent grounding with fundamental principles.

Alternately, for those who have read the first two books, the summary will serve to foster more profound understanding of Body-Self or Soma-Self and Mind-Self or Cognitive-Self interrelationships and cooperative functioning.

Body-Self

Body-Self is equipped with multiple sensory-arrays. Each variant is specifically designed to accept only its own particular narrow frequency range at its event-horizon from the unrelenting 24/7 Bombardment (if needed reference *Way Better* Your L.I.F.E^2.: **Body-Self** Detailed Discussions section DD-001).

Conclusively then, Sensory event-horizons provide the **fodder**, which provisions a 'glimpses' of what is going on **Out-There**.

Way Better Your L.I.F.E^2.: Body-Self utilized the Soma-Self model (see Illustration Section: item IS-102) to visually detail the many **Components** responsible for manipulation and reformulation of sensory-accepted information into tailored **data-streams.** Components include Inception-Filter, Recognition-Assessment, Intensity-Assessment, Threat-Check, Soma-Survival, Soma-Slotting, Soma-Response and Soma-Actions.

Additionally introduced during explanations of Component functionality were constructs and concepts such as Soma sensory-acceptance, Tags, data-morphing, Tag-Clusters, data-archiving, recognition plus others.

Also explained in detail was that each Body-Self sensory-system has its specific destination or data-archive termination-point in its particular dedicated brain-mass or Matched-Base-Frequency.

Clarifications of the variances between the Self-Duo (Body-Self and Mind-Self) exposed not only Cognitive-Self's **neural real-estate** as far more extensive and complex than Soma-Self's but also the many reasons why this is so.

The complexity contrast between Self-Duo is suggested by the books different covers. The *Way Better* Your L.I.F.E^2.: Body-Self book cover depicts a simpler, less complicated, black-and-white neural-matrix. *Way Better* Your L.I.F.E^2.: Mind-Self cover on the other hand displays a complex, multi-colored neural-array. It is intended to indicate a much more intricate and multifaceted resource.

Defining their contrasts is important because distinctions explain not only Body-Self's reliance on Soma habitual-response as its primary rapid-response strategy but also the incredible **Figure-It-Out** capabilities of **Cognitive-Complex**, which assists Soma-Self by discovering **The-Ways** and deploying best-case **Test-It** action **Solution** scenarios.

Even though incredibly useful for survival, Soma-Self data-archive population to the point of effectively moving the body (Soma) away from recognized impacting external events can not only require years to become viable but also require special training for Soma-Self to evolve sufficiently to render superior instant habitual-responses.

For instance, athletes like Olympic slalom skiers, through extensive training regimens can super populate data-archives and thus induce habitual-responses that 'automatically' determine best-case scenario as they speed down a mountainside course.

Incredibly, even if some data-archives are extensively populated, Soma-Self responsive habits are tenaciously specific and do not typically cross-pollinate. For instance, acquiring a skill with your right hand does not spontaneously make for comparable left-handed ability.

This is because the Matched-Base-Frequency data-archives being populated for the right hand and are frequency different to those of the left hand due to Location-ID frequency information being incorporated into tens of thousands of 'right hand' **Tags**.

> Professional musicians are also excellent examples. They know without a doubt that daily practice is necessary to not only hone and broaden intricate habitual-skills but also keep them from fading.

Thus, recognition and appropriate outbound or response **Tactics** of sensory-accepted Bombardment-Sphere impacts must wait for sufficient sensory-data population of its Soma-Self Matched-Base-Frequency data-archives to be usefully referenceable. Prominently, if a child is to survive, many years of others keeping the youngster safe are necessary.

> Importantly, even though both Self-Duo partners (Body-Self and Mind-Self) provision habitual-responses, they are substantively different.

Intriguingly, although Body-Self habitual-responses ultimately work well for 'recognized' or previously encountered events of low intensity, Body-Self neural-array design is severely lacking when **UN-recognized** and/or **higher-intensity** events occur.

> Consequently, book-one also detailed how Body-Self's Threat, Trend and Survival evaluators deploy to ascertain when a Bombardment-event is **problematic** and thus beyond Soma-Self's range of capabilities.

Fortunately - to our great advantage - for anything but 'recognized-and-low-intensity' situations, Body-Self (depending on conditions) creates one or the other of two **Cognitive-Alert** data-packages: a **request-alert** or an **imperative-alert**.

Variously composed of morphed action-potentials of both a current-new 'problematic' Deluge event and analogous retrieved data-archive fodder, a Cognitive-Alert is transmitted to prompt event-resolution assistance from Cognitive-Self: Body-Self's Self-Duo collaborator.

Specifically, a Cognitive-Alert is tailored by applicable Soma-Self mechanisms for either possible 'problematic' condition. Specifically, when survival is not at stake, Threat-Check generates a request-alert: when survival may be at stake, Soma-Survival fashions a more complex imperative-alert.

Mind-Self

Book-two, *Way Better* Your L.I.F.E.^{2}.: Mind-Self discussions begin at the Cluster-**Works** in-box for Body-Self's Cognitive-Alerts. Note that subsequent discussions assume the in-box has just been populated with one of Soma-Self two varying intensity Cognitive-Alert data-packets.

This 'triggering-event', which alerts Mind-Self that Body-Self is requesting assistance for a 'problematic' issue is immediately intensity-assessed by Cognitive-Filters **Cluster-Works** evaluation-processor array.

Pivotally, Cluster-Works intensity assessment is the first 'step' toward ascertaining the appropriate **Figure-It-Out** Cognitive-Pathway to be utilized for **Solutioning**: from Nominal CP-5 to Survival CP-1 (see illustration section: 'Cognitive-Pathways Model' item IS-103).

Resultantly, when Cognitive-Alert intensity is sufficient to engage Cognitive-Pathway Three (CP-3), Figure-It-Out, in order to gather additional information about what is going on Out-There brings its proactive visual sensor-array to bear.

Importantly, CP-3 is the first 'Cognitive-Pathway' to engage proactive Cognitive-Sensors (vision).

Vision or **Visual-Sensors** are remarkable because they deliver massive additional information of a different nature than do Body or Soma-sensors.

It would not be useful to process Cognitive-Alerts in isolation from the very visual-data that is being gathered to assist in resolution of a 'problematic' issue.

Therefore, it falls on **Cross-Sensory-Bundling** to perform integration-assessment. Its evaluation is designed to determine data-elements that 'match' between a Cognitive-Alert and a **Visual-Works** event-data packet.

> More specifically, as visual (Cognitive-Sensor) data-events pour in via **Visual-Works**, they are applicably integrated by Cross-Sensory-Bundling with Cluster-Works data-bundles (originally inspired by Cognitive-Alerts) thus enabling exacting symmetry and collaboration between the Soma-Self and Cognitive-Self sensory systems.

As the cyclical cooperative continues, all Cross-Sensory-Bundling matched and integrated data-bundles are once again intensity assessed and propagated toward either **NORM** or **PRIORITY** channels (see Cognitive-Pathways Model illustration IS-103).

Cross-Sensory-Bundling is additionally pivotal then as it enables Figure-It-Out to choose an intensity appropriate Cognitive-Pathway. In other words, depending on the integrated intensity of the Cognitive-Alert either alone or in combination with data provided by visual-sensors, one of five Cognitive-Pathways is engaged.

> Cognitive-Pathway determination also ensures best allocation of neurological processing resources.

Consequently, cognitive resources both entirely focus on the 'problematic' Bombardment-event and initialize appropriate-to-event **E-Puzzles** that are the foundation for effective Solutioning.

Visual sensor-arrays discussed above are actually engaged by CP-3's **Template-Processor**. It in turn engages CP-3's **Considered-Response** mechanism (see Cognitive-Pathways diagram). This amazing cooperative is purposed to morph sensory-data and store resulting 'Harmonic' action-potentials in their own specialized data-repositories.

Integration, 'Harmonic-repositories' and rapid retrieval are critical to ensure one's physical movements are executed quickly and smoothly by the retrieval recognized patterns.

Otherwise, if neural-arrays were not capable of 'harmonic-pattern' retention, the thousands of tiny movements one makes every second would have to be figured out separately. We would not be human at that point but more like a clam.

Efficiently and effectively Cognitive-Pathway outbound to Soma-Self data-packages or **Test-Its**, which are created by Parameter-Processor and/or Cognition-Complex propel Soma-Self positional change within one's **Bombardment-Sphere** in order to respond physical systems and keep us safe. In other words, positional change is accomplished by Test-Its activating physical structures (muscles, etc.).

Thus, do one of the five types of Figure-It-Out Test-Its incrementally direct one to 'best possible outcome': for not only recognized / higher-intensity and unrecognized / nominal-intensity sensory-events but also unrecognized and high-intensity events.

Incredibly, Test-Its also spirit new sensory-feedback in a cyclical Self-Duo dance designed to interactively keep us safe: by not only deploying Mind-Self response-patterns but also provisioning fodder for Puzzle Solutioning.

> Cognitive-Pathway processing mechanisms account for the vast majority of Cognitive-Self Module data-morphing: from retention in many types of data-archives to Puzzle creation and comparative recall to manifestation as cognitive habitual-responses, responsive-behaviors, awareness, chosen actions and individualized perception of reality.

Ultimately, as childhood inexorably migrates toward 'maturity', it is highest complexity Tier-Five **Reference-Complex** Experience-Senses or Cognitive-Habits, which furnish the full array of one's beliefs and attitudes.

> This point is critical as it is one's Cognitive-Habits, even when 2 or 3 years old, that intercede as a primary filter directly moderating Puzzle Solutioning and therefore one's living-experiences.

In other words, Cognitive-Habits triggered because of **frequency-similarity** to either current-new and/or Devise-Mulling dredged up archived-old are always those with the largest significantly-similar action-potentials. Therefore, they are the **GO-TO** chaos-habits and pro-habits.

> 'Filtering' outcome is thus a direct consequence of the intensity of **frequency-relevant** Experience-Sense action-potentials.

For instance, if extremely frightened by a serious fall, resulting Experience-Senses would be high-intensity because the action-potential in corresponding Tier 5 data-archives would be very 'large'.

Thus, if presented with the option of bungee jumping, although the thought might entice, frequency related Cognitive-Habits would immediately filter current-new and attempt to change sensory-acceptance.

In other words, Cognitive-Habits bent on risk-avoidance would take control and adjust current-new by firing intense streams of **Test-It**s, which would cause reactions such as 'a sick feeling in the pit of your stomach', sweating, extreme nervousness, disturbing mind-images, etc.

Additionally, **Test-It**s will thus change sensory-acceptance by changing position in your Bombardment-Sphere: i.e., **Test-It**s will quickly back you away from the edge of the bridge. Cognitive-Habits thus change life-experiences.

> Experience-Senses become synonymous with observable and consistent actions, behaviours or Cognitive-Habits, which observers simplify as one's personality.

Cognitive-Self habitual-responses, including Experience-Senses, such as beliefs, derive in abundant, varied and elastic cognitive neural-resources.

It is in this amazing neural-matrix that the Soma-Self survival-mandate is expanded into a Cognitive-Self survival-mandate to Figure-It-Out and ensure best possible outcome (The-Ways): not just survival, as for Soma-Self, but chosen broader-scope enhanced **living-conditions**.

This point is critical because as you will come to understand in discussions below, expectations, which are actually Cognitive-Habits, especially when compromised due to low self-esteem, keep us from pursuing better living-conditions by keeping us from gathering new experiences.

Therefore, the result is same-old, same-old, which, in this authors opinion is not living but subsisting.

> Remarkable is when sensory-events are **sufficiently-intense** because this evokes Cognition-Complex's **Delving-Trio** to engage. This leap is vitally

important because Cognition-Complex is one's ticket to choice and thus Living-in-Full-Experience-and-Excitement: L.I.F.E^2.

Better Living-Condition Activation

Delving-Trio is miraculous because each of its three members (Targeted, Ranged and Extensive-Delving) can spirit intensity appropriate cognitive-responses and correspondingly balanced situational awareness. Their activation is earmarked by the deployment of ever more complex outbound Feedback-Loop Test-It's, which are designed to assess Solutioning progress.

Solutioning progress monitoring is possible because as Test-Its change one's position within their Bombardment-Sphere, different 'ongoing-until-resolved' sensory-data is thereby gathered. In this instance 'resolved' means a drop back to **nominal** status as a corresponding Solution to Puzzles is accomplished.

Excitement Cycle

Here are the reasons why being 'jacked-up' (passionate) will help you both discover and fulfill your passions.

The greater the **UN**-recognized and/or higher-intensity activities within your Bombardment-Sphere, the more Puzzles are created.

The more Puzzles created, the more are solved.

The more solved, the greater the experiences: thus the more excited you are.

Moreover, the more excited you are the more pronounced are experiences, due to an increase in the potency of action-potentials within Cognitive-Self data-archives.

The greater the experiences, the greater the likelihood you will be **DO**ing significantly-similar activities again. The more you **DO** exciting activities, the more Puzzles and thus one continues to be active within their Bombardment-Sphere.

Game Changing

Remarkably, although Cognitive-Self always responds to Soma-Self Cognitive-Alerts, the Devise-Mulling powerhouse is also engaged by Cognitive-Sensors alerting a **remarkable-feature**.

In other words, Visual processors alone can provide adequate intensity to Cross-Sensory-Bundling to ensure the engagement of either Cognitive-Pathway 3 or higher.

> Engagement of CP-3 is significant because its process-tree enables proactive avoidance.

Remarkably, Figure-It-Out massively extends Soma-Self capabilities by providing an incredible **game-changing** processing-platform termed **Devise-Mulling** that is designed for independent processing activities: i.e. retrieval from archived-old without the need for current-new as an inspirator.

Incredibly, its **Mulling** activities, which one typically refers to as consciousness, pondering or thinking can operate either stealthfully as in dreams and/or overtly as in conscious chosen interaction.

Overt actions are accomplished by yet another game-changing cognitive capability: Regardless of conscious state, Devise-Mulling can create not only Puzzles to get answers but also **Test-IT**s to spirit sensory-feedback.

> Recall that Test-Its suggest action-plans tailored to prompt Soma-Sensors and/or Visual-Sensors to provide sensory-feedback purposed to enrich and speed-up resolution.

In other words, in order to clear unresolved Puzzles, Devise-Mulling continually scrutinises to evaluate Puzzle resolution-status.

Devise-Mulling accomplishes this incredible Puzzle-reconciliation process by ferreting cognitive data-archives - whether physically awake or not - in order to contribute Puzzle answers or F-Puzzles.

Notably, the larger an E-Puzzle the greater is its action-potential: whether a consequence of either current-new contribution and/or its accumulation due to being updated by Devise-Mulling ferreting archived-old.

As we now know, the greater a Puzzles action-potential, the greater the **mulling-pressure** to resolve the Puzzle because it becomes the primary **GO-TO**.

Recall each Devise-Mulling 'pass' also builds corresponding entries in its dedicated DM-Assembly data-archive.

This build-up contributes to mulling-pressure as well because it makes the combination of Puzzle and linked DM-Assembly large enough to attract most of the pathway attention and therefore the majority of the available processing time and energy resources.

The consequence of intense sensory-acceptance is that Puzzles, which are not part of the current-new frequency-flow do not get resolved as quickly.

If sustained, as in combat conditions, this can become a significantly debilitating issue. This is because the build-up of unresolved Puzzles can make for not only a stressful day as unresolved thoughts keep Chatterboxing in one's mind but also restless sleep and vivid dreams as Devise-Mulling seeks resolution of un-answered Puzzles by dredging through data-archives.

Integrating and virtually animating all aspects of the copious quantities of variant data-flow from both Cognitive-Alerts and Visual-Sensors is the responsibility of the **Movie-of-Your-Life** presentation center.

It is continually hard at work ensuring holistic continuity of one's reality experience. Fortuitously and incredibly, the Movie-of-Your-Life production is mandated to virtually present one's reality without interruption, sputtering's, pauses or blank spots.

> In this amazing Movie-of-Your-Life facility, 'remarkable-features' from both Cognitive-Alerts and Visual-Sensors are superimposed over background CP-5 and CP-4 Soma-Sensor and Cognitive-Sensor data-flows to present one a virtual mosaic of continuous and situationally appropriate, yet integrated event-progression over a synchronous flowing backdrop.

Pro-Habit Creation Environment

Indubitably, from 'How-We-Work' explanations in *Way Better* Your L.I.F.E^2.: Body-Self and *Way Better* Your L.I.F.E^2.: **Mind**, one can rely on the following truth.

Everything one is and everything one can become or is going to be is a direct consequence of diverse data-archive contents, which have been or will be populated (after mechanism manipulations) by various initializing sensory-accepted events from one's Bombardment-Sphere.

> This precept is incredibly significant because sensory-acceptance is thus established as the initiation or touch-point for 100% of everything one now knows; or will ever know.

More explicitly, when Tolerable-Signal and Threshold-Potential are suitable, sensory-acceptance is a direct consequence of sensory-receptor neurons accepting certain ranges of frequency-based Bombardment-Sphere events.

> Sensory-acceptance thereby initiates a **data-acquisition cycle**, which through 'recognition' analysis culminates in the storage of morphed action-potential or **fodder** in a variety of data-archives purposed to enhance both survival prospects and enhanced living-conditions.

Living-Experience Amplification

Stands to reason then, data-archive comparative reference site content is expandable. Specifically, scope or broader data-references can be either added to or accelerated by altering one's Bombardment-Sphere activities to provide conditions, which are more favorable.

Additionally and incredibly, with the amendment of sufficient Bombardment-Sphere conditions, even Experience-Senses or Cognitive-Habits and therefore one's **living-experience** can be substantially augmented by the creation of new pro-habits.

> At this point, you might be thinking it's obvious **living-perspectives** can change if one transforms their attitudes and activities.

Puzzle is how can adjustment be achieved consistently and with minimal effort?

All have been gifted with dual habitual-natures for a purpose (Soma-Habits and Cognitive-Habits). Specifically, to allow quick navigation through recognized low-intensity events when initiated by Soma-self and effect proactive avoidance in **UN**-recognized and/or higher-intensity Cognitive-Self handled events.

This strategy works because it effectively enhances survival-potential by not only minimizing redundancy of effort but also freeing up limited neural-processing real-estate for **problematic** issues.

> Without doubt, one is at greatest risk in 'new' situations because slow response means survival-potential is decreased, thereby reciprocally increasing danger.

'Recognition' on the other hand, enables rapid deployment of both Soma-Habit and/or Cognitive-Habit patterned-actions from applicable data-archives, which thereby spirit appropriate physical structures into action, which thus move one toward safety and/or improved conditions (ideally).

> In other words, a 'recognized' Bombardment-event does not require time-consuming and process-resource gobbling re-evaluation by Soma-self and Cognitive-Self. Instead, Habitual patterned-responses facilitate rapid, survival-potential enhancing physical action.

However, to **create new pro-habits and not let your old chaos-habits continue to create you**…attitude and activity, two somewhat controllable habits, need to be addressed in the opposite order: first activity, then attitude.

Activity must occur first because it alone is the sole provisioner of 'fodder'. Only then will consequent and symmetrical attitude morphing be possible.

> Order is significant because what is required to create new attitudes, Experience-Senses or Cognitive-Habits is an adjustment of activity to **UN**-recognized, intensified **DO**ing: i.e., Living-in-Full-Experience-and-Excitement as much as possible.

Critical: Cognitive chaos-habits are currently responsible for limiting, blinkering or **reduction-filtering** your true options by impeding you from **DO**ing Bombardment-Sphere adjustments that would be more beneficial.

Take 100 random people…some live in scarcity; most are glad they have something: yet some have plenty. Why does this attitude variance exist?

> Those with plenty typically realize all prizes are there for picking off the **Conveyor-Belt of LIFE.**

Actually then, whatever you **TRULY** want is just your perception away.

However, mandatory prerequisites to pick from the Conveyor-Belt of L.I.F.E^2 are the pro-habit Experience-Sense attitudes that you are worthy, capable and attainment is absolutely possible for you.

As positive attitudes are Cognitive Pro-Habits, they can be acquired by creating them: Not only that but their chaos-habits opposites can absolutely be relegated to oblivion.

> Today choose to both create pro-habits and stop giving **creating-you** permission to your chaos-habits.

Want-Dreams

When you don't daydream and/or night-dream about the life and things you TRULY want, you are not going to be able to make them come true. This is because minimal Puzzles will be available for Devise-Mulling to Solution.

Devise-Mulling creates Puzzles when you are conceptualizing or dreaming about what you want. The great news is that Devise-Mulling, to resolve these Puzzles, also creates Test-It's that absolutely direct the gathering of applicable fodder from the Out-There.

Additionally and powerfully though, the existence of E-Puzzles enables normally bypassed action-potentials to 'stick' by attaching them as F-Puzzles to all your dream created E-Puzzles.

Thus, the more you **DO**, regardless of what it is, the quicker will your **want-dreams** will be actualized and become part of your reality: this is How-We-Work.

Important to remember then, to enable Devise-Mulling to fulfill its mandate to **Solution Puzzles** and find **The-Ways** fodder **P-Cluster** (Puzzles) and other data-archives by activity or **DO**ing.

Synchronistically, while you are **DO**ing and thus gathering fodder in order to fulfill your want-dreams, you are simultaneously not only creating new pro-habits, which are aligned with getting you your want-dreams but also inactivating chaos-habits by redirecting fodder, normally destined toward their data-archive arrays, to pro-habits instead.

> Thus, the more you **DO** and the more and grander your want-dreams, the faster your pro-habits will transparently work away on your behalf to fulfill them: this is without a doubt their designed nature – to get you what you TRULY want. It's How-We-Work!

Incredibly, even if you do not currently have prominent want-dreams or passions to fulfill, you certainly will when you start **DO**ing.

It does not even matter what you start **DO**ing because action breeds action. This is because the two automatic consequences of DOing is that Puzzles are created and that Devise-Mulling will go to work Solutioning. It's How-We-Work!

> This author considers **DO** to be the most powerful word in the English language because without **DO**ing one can actualize nothing!

Remember, it is UN-recognized and higher-intensity fodder, which massively kicks Devise-Mulling into significant action.

Wonderfully, Devise-Mulling's awesome power 'Mulls' and Solutions 24/7: for the specific purpose of Solutioning and getting you what you want.

> Incredible as well, the pro-habit of just 'starting' to **DO** something new will fodder so much action-potential that you will soon become so excited about the many possibilities, there will not seem time to **DO** it all.

Bombardment-Sphere adjustments are critically important because altered Bombardment-Sphere positioning is the **key** to inspiring new sensory-accepted events, which as a direct consequence begins the creation of new pro-habits and thus morphed perspective.

> After all … It is not your creating acceptable from plenty that will fuel Devise-Mulling excitement: but instead your striving to create awesome from scarcity.

Allow me to explain differently. From infancy through at least early adolescence, encompassing a few quashed rebellions at about age two, eight and twelve, most everyone was domesticated by others who were domesticated before them.

> I state domesticated because true choice was not an option. This is incontrovertible as the requirements and points-of-view of others repetitively and perhaps emphatically filled one's young days.

As a typical youngster, you had neither the option of unbiased flexible opinions nor the latitude to try out all the possibilities you wanted without interference. Thousands of times in your childhood, you were taken away from things you passionately wanted to explore.

> Huge kudos to any mentors who consistently not only accepted and allowed inquisitiveness but also provided broad-scope options.

So typical 'growing-up' was really in an environment where **in the absence of good comparable information, any information seemed good**. Thus, restricted and not necessarily 'best' Deluge was sensory-accepted into your data-archives: thus, it initiated the creation of Habits; some useful, some destructive.

Resultantly, one's Tier-one through Tier-four data-archives and more complex Tier-five Experience-Senses, which present as attitudes and beliefs, were populated with sensory input formulated and regulated by others: no matter how well intentioned.

No wonder locking ourselves in our bedroom, getting away on a bike ride or a solitary drive seemed such a treat.

> As others mostly controlled one's Bombardment-Sphere at home, at school and at play, one's range of sensory-information was restricted: therefore, attitudes and behaviours manifested accordingly limited.

However, here is the great news: You can stop your domesticated **chaos-habits** from continuing to create you.

As you have not only survived childhood but also understand How-We-Work you are now in a position to create your own **pro-habits** from new information you choose appropriate and applicable; then relegate those old chaos-habits, which were built from biased fodder, on the back burner.

In other words in Force-of-Habit terms, populate new data-archives with significantly higher action-potentials, which will resultantly (as this is How-We-Work!) become the **GO-TO** pro-habit instead.

> Habits play us up to 95% of the day anyway: so design yours to get you what you want.

Now you are 'in-the-know', not only can you create your own pro-habits but also they can become your ever-vigilant friend. As such, they will continue to get you what you **TRULY** want.

> The word 'truly' is in the phrase because you cannot fake it: you simply cannot 'trick' your brain…if you are not 100% committed minimal new-creation will occur and consequently chaos-habits will persist.

Importantly, creating a pro-habit does not immediately make it the GO-TO de facto be-all and end-all: other attention is necessary. This is because old-habits, you know those domesticated chaos-ones, have had years of action-potentials added to their multi-tiers of data-archives making them huge and pervasive.

After all, from the perspective of action-potential populated, neural-arena brain-mass, a new pro-habit is only a small player initially.

In other words, the data-element action-potentials comprising its substance within various neurons within applicable neural data-archives initially only house miniscule action-potentials.

> Notably, the created new pro-habit is as well subject to the pervasive universe law of **high energy always supersedes lower energy** (recall the 'candle in the sunshine' example in book two where the candle in a dark room was sufficient to slightly illuminate the room but had no effect in the sunshine).

In other words, this means the new pro-habit is not 'huge and pervasive' but small and fledgling.

Therefore, unless **TRULY** want is in place, which is the power of emotion, intensity or passion, which is also the driver for data-archive creation and retrieval…voila the old chaos-habit sets kick back in because they literally do have the superseding or overriding power.

Reminder: data-archives are populated for a reason…as a comparative for current-data. Thus, recognition results in habitual tried-and-true rapid responses being deployed to enhance survival potential instead of much slower Cognitive evaluative cyclical-feedback whose slowness could spell disaster.

Resultantly, as survival is always the main impetus for Habit creation old-habits never, never, never totally go away.

Chaos-habit sets like addictions are hard to shake because their action-potentials are so large that they can stubbornly remain the GO-TO's when surroundings (Bombardment-Sphere) and events are recognized or familiar.

However, with enough diligence toward practicing a new pro-habit, its action-potential will grow larger than the old chaos-habit's action-potential and therefore, due to it having the overriding power, become the GO-TO preference instead.

Critical Key: Both new pro-habit creation and practice require keeping surrounding aspects at least slightly **UN-recognized** and more intense. These conditions are critical to add additional chosen fodder to fledgling Tier-One through Tier-Five Cognitive-Self data-archives while **DO**ing.

Neural Real-Estate Scarcity

Additionally beneficial, although it would not seem so at first glance is scarcity of neural 'real-estate'. Fortuitously, when push-comes-to-shove, neurons within data-archives, not refreshed by use are targets for recycling.

In other words, **out with the old and in with the new** is the neurological standard when **neural shelf-space** becomes scarce: actually, this is a main reason one forgets bits of stuff.

In other words, when an old chaos-habit is not being used and therefore not being updated by fresh action-potentials, some of the neurons housing its action-potentials will be appropriated and reused.

This recycling methodology is great when creating and practicing new pro-habits, but a tad annoying when heading out on the tennis court for the first time in the summer and experiencing being rusty.

'Rusty' means some neuron action-potentials of some responsible data-archive neurons have been usurped for other uses during the winter pause.

In other words, due to lack of use (i.e., no new significantly-similar action-potentials), some archive neurons were freed-up for different current action-potential requirements.

> Be clear though, only some of the chaos-habit neural real-estate will be reused: not all of it.

Resultantly, one must remain diligent until new pro-habits are strongly established by copious action-potentials, which were of course derived from much **DO**ing.

> When a higher action-potential data-archive is realized, the likelihood of regression to old behaviours is less likely.

This is so because practice has established the new pro-habit data-archive neurons with significantly larger action-potentials. Upon recall, the higher action-potentials become the GO-TO: i.e., they are actioned instead. It's How-We-Work!

The situation then is as follows: by the time one is twenty-something, habits drive 95% of one's day. Most habits were created not by choice and due diligence but by domestication. The essential purpose of habits is to keep us safe via recognition processing, which drives us, like water, down the middle of a right-angled wooden 'flume'.

Habits due to their repetitive deployment have large action-potentials making them the rapid GO-TO action inducer in recognized and low-intensity situations: whereas existing Experience-Sense or Cognitive-Habits control perspective in UN-recognized and/or higher-intensity situations.

> Critical to reiterate is habits are fixed: they cannot be changed.

However, new habits can be created from new information through choice. Intriguingly, carefully designed new pro-habits can be your 'best-friend' automatically getting you what you most truly want.

> Now you know How-We-Work, it is absolutely possible to intercede.

In other words, it is in your **choice-power** to re-invent yourself or re-become by **DO**ing many different chosen things.

Remember, created pro-habits repetitively and unquestioningly will do your bidding: this is after all their intrinsic design.

Action is Key

Action or **DO**ing is a vital Key to creating new pro-habit powers because activity literally creates new data-archives or Brackets. Synchronistically however, both the intensity and duration of **DO**ing increment even greater action-potentials or sensory-experience bases.

Notably then, to create powerful new **Force-of-Habits**, passionate **DO**ing for extended intervals is pivotal because dramatic activity **fodders** the expansive data-archives necessary to ensure they become the **GO-TO**'s.

Remember, greater action-potential ensures superior and preferential recall.

Therefore…Don't be afraid to massively action your day-dreams!

Active engagement is mandatory for another reason: it causes the manifestation of higher intensity and/or UN-recognized events. These of course are the additional requirements to engage Cognition-Complex at the Cognitive-Pathway 3 or higher levels, which resultantly induces Visual-Sensors and enables awareness and conscious choice.

Individually, **UN**-recognized or higher-intensity are good conditions. This is because when either is in play they will more fully populate both Soma-Self and Cognitive-Self data-archives. It's How-We-Work!

However, when both are simultaneously activated by passionate **DO**ing, they will fast-track your objectives because when intensity is high enough, Cognition-Complex will also be alerted by Parameter-Processor.

Recall, Cognition-Complex is what turns Visual-Sensors on. Their activation results in not only enhancing action-potentials by additionally populating data-archives but also inspiring several enhanced complexity Test-It recommendations. As we now know Test-Its are tailored to change Bombardment-Sphere position and thus gather broader-scope feedback to aid more rapid **Solutioning**.

Visual cues are neurologically potent! They provide upwards of 85% of the sensory information in unfamiliar situations. Therefore, when creating new pro-habits a change of scenery will dramatically enable new: whereas same-old, same-old scenery will incapacitate new and only serve to maintain old chaos-habits.

> Vastly important then is to understand that greater action-potential definitely makes it more likely that pro-habit patterns formed from copious activity will become the GO-TO ones: and thus bypass a chaos-habit of lesser action-potential.

Thus, without Cognition-Complex involvement chaos-habits will continue to operate and carry on creating you.

What actions are necessary to create pro-habits?

First, you must determine with **conviction**, which of your chaos-habits are not getting you what you **TRULY** want. Remember, conviction is critical because emotion is the power-driver for both data-archiving (action-potential storage) and recall.

> Don't even try to trick yourself through justifications or self-manipulations: that just won't work.

Next, decide on what you want. The vision does not need to be precise at the start as one truly does not know the end-point or destination until many trials (data-archive population or experience acquisitions) have been attempted: direction will therefore suffice.

> For example, if you want to learn self-defence become excited about the reasons for your conviction and begin a program immediately: for instance, by scoping out appropriate instruction facilities.

If you do not want to begin right away then your passion is just not sufficient to carry you through.

So find something you are **compelled to DO** without procrastination: which by the way is a chaos-habit worthy of being delegated to the neurological recycling bin.

Finally, use Devise-Mulling to name and create a new pro-habit in-progress **Puzzle** (you can have as many as you like) with features you currently think would be most useful.

Don't worry too much about precise content because as new information arrives, due to your extensive involvement or passionate **DO**ing, you can later choose to adjust and/or add to Puzzles until you are satisfied with content.

> More specifically, by actively and intensity engaging unfamiliar (UN-recognized) aspects within your Bombardment-Sphere you can create and then adjust individual **Puzzles.**

Resultantly, depending on both Test-It induced actions and Experience-Senses (Cognitive-Habits) filtering, two aspects for which one can exert some control, you get to: create your own (new) pro-habits; continually tune them by **DO**ing; and by inactivity demote old chaos-habits.

> When asked by someone how you are faring, you can now respond by stating either I have a few chaos-habits that need diminishing or, when all is going as you have created, you can confidently reply that my pro-habits are TRULY working for me, thank you.

Knowing How-We-Work is great: however, understanding how to apply this expertise to Living-In-Full-Experience-and-Excitement (coined **L.I.F.E^2.** in *Way Better* Your L.I.F.E^2.: **Mind**) is even better.

This being so, let's first expose some worst habits: their domestication origins, limitations, etc. then define how each can be usurped by creating more useful and dynamic pro-habits fully supportive of enacting your particular wants and dreams.

Let's start at **The-Way-One-Thinks** as it encompasses some of our worst chaos-habits.

Worst Habits

Every millisecond of every day one's living-experience is impelled by two immutable forces that intersect with randomly presented Deluge events at one's event-horizons: Habit driven reactions and Test-It directives.

More specifically, we are inescapably driven by four absolutes that deploy cyclically like the seasons.

Four Absolutes

First, various Soma-Self and Cognitive-Self sensory-array neurons are obliged to accept their specific frequency-delegated ration of the 24/7 Deluge.

Next, follow-on mechanisms are required to transfer, apportion, process, evaluate and data-archive **fodder.**

Thirdly, response mechanisms are designed to rapidly re-join incoming action-potential frequencies with most closely matched tried-and-true habitual-response patterns.

Finally, Test-It's are delegated to produce cyclical outbound prompts to inspire additional sensory-feedback purposed for Solutioning Puzzles.

Notably, accumulation and storage of sensory-accepted **fodder** from Out-There is indispensable.

'Fodder' is essential because 100% of not only one's current understandings, beliefs, behaviours and 'personalities' have been derived from sensory-accepted events being processed and then data-archived but also one's future changes to current attitudes will be likewise derived from it.

One's day is driven by Habits and Test-Its. Habits encompass breathing, swallowing, dressing, walking, eating, driving, parking, thinking, speaking and so on.

Test-It's spirit the mandate to cyclically **Figure-It-Out** by changing one's position in their Bombardment-Sphere. Their action directives resultantly collect feedback via the provision of new frequency-appropriate sensory-data until cognitive resolution for a 'problematic-issue' (Puzzle) is accomplished.

> More simply put Test-It's are purposed to try this and that, then another this, to see if they work wholly or partially.

Seriously, do not underestimate the incredible ongoing utility of automated Habits as both Soma-Habits and Cognitive-Habits are pivotal to not only survival but also daily functioning as well as the ongoing enactment of enhanced living-conditions.

Fortunately, when one creates pro-habits, these more useful Habits will also continue to fulfill their GO-TO mandates without any intervention or additional effort. It's How-We-Work!

> Pro-habits that get us what we want are like the best Butler ever.

Good news: pro-habit creation is not hard.

Firstly, it is possible for one to choose Bombardment-Sphere conditions, which are more conducive to rapidly building pro-habit action-potential arsenals.

> One's Bombardment-Sphere is as if you are a big target … So, better to make yourself a target for gifts, than for missiles.

Way Better Your L.I.F.E².: Mind-Self elucidated that Devise-Mulling can not only create its own Solutioning Puzzles but also send its own specialized cyclical **Test-**

IT's to inspire Soma-Self (or Body-self) positional adjustments and thus gather feedback regarding its Solutioning progress (i.e., by resolving CP-Sets; i.e., filling-in F-Puzzles answers).

So if **DO**ing new events by changing one's Bombardment-Sphere is such a big deal, what stops us from getting out there, experimenting and '**DO**ing' all the time?

> In fact, when Habitual autopilots are pervasive, life is mundane.

> Conversely, life is exciting when one's Bombardment-Sphere presents new and/or escalated intensity.

The answer to the question above resides with one of our worst domesticated chaos-habit sets: **The-Way-We-Think**.

In other words, Cognitive-Habits housed in the Tier-5 pinnacle data-archive shelter several core habit-sets, which drive our **living-experiences**. Topping the list of Cognitive-Habits and at the very core of one's reality is **The-Way-We-Think**.

Of course, Habits, like almost everything else in the universe exist on a gradient: in this case from destructive to constructive. Therefore, it is imperative to identify worst habits first, so they can be rectified.

In addition, as habits do not exist independently but have tendrils that trigger other Habit-sets, rectification, when this major not-so-useful chaos-habit set is active will additionally have positive repercussions for connected conspirators.

The-Way-We-Think

Useful or not useful, **The-Way-We-Think** literally provisions ones most significant Cognitive-Habit drivers: these include, worthiness or confidence in self, self-doubt, beliefs, attitudes, preferences, hates, biases and the list goes on.

I understand most have probably never considered The-Way-We-Think to be a Habit, let alone a potentially worst Cognitive-Habit.

However, no doubt The-Way-We-Think and its closely linked **The-Way-We-Speak** are actually one's most highly domesticated Habits. Understandably, the way one thinks drives not only perceptions but also actions such as how we speak.

The problem is once we fixate on thinking and speaking a certain way, perceptions consequently become severely limited.

Limited perceptions are like muting your senses: except 'senses' are receiving just fine and not the issue.

Actually, the true culprit is incorporation of **current-new** with chaos-habit GO-TO **Experience-Senses** by Devise-Mulling that inhibits accurate perception: More on that topic later.

So, how did chaos-habit perceptions get their enormous power?

From your Mothers first 'hello little one' through school and university and beyond into the workplace, one is domesticated on how to think and speak.

Consider the last time you were thinking or speaking: was it necessary to consciously construct the rapidly presenting virtual symbols, words and/or pictures?

Of course not: This is because these capabilities are cognitive-habits that are being inspired by higher-intensity Cognition-Complex **Ranged-Delving** and more-intense **Extensive-Delving** situations.

When passion or intensity is sufficiently elevated, Outbound Test-It's may also include Devise-Mulling assemblages (**Test-IT**'s), which one senses as inspiration.

In fact, capability may not have as much to do with neural real-estate availability as it does with Cognitive-Habits or Experience-Senses, which domestication honed to dictate belief in your limitations, instead of in your expansive aptitudes.

Unless inspired by higher-intensity, one simply has nothing to say:
When massively passionate, one cannot say enough.

Where might data-archiving become restrictive rather than expansive?

Developmentally speaking, from birth (and perhaps before) and on into pre-teens everyone was influenced to various degrees by the attitudes, concepts, dictates and contrived situations created by others (hopefully well intentioned; not manipulative) that passed in-and-out of one's Bombardment-Sphere.

Resultantly, as one's Bombardment-Sphere was mostly moulded by others, one thus becomes domesticated by individuals who were actually domesticated by others who were domesticated before them.

Thus, many traits and huge handfuls of beliefs and attitudes track through generations.

> Being domesticated by others who were domesticated before is a cycle that dates back tens-of-thousands of years.

As our species requires extensive nurturing by others for survival, domestication came about innocently enough.

However, its deployment has very limiting side effects: specifically … compromised sensory-foddering, which leads to corralled perceptions.

> Domestication also massively affects self-esteem. Notable is when influential others determine a child's spirit and inquisitiveness an unacceptable nuisance and further determine the youngsters energy as an obnoxious condition to be tamed and eliminated.

Resultantly, through at least 50 plus millennia, as tribes and evolving societies believed their way was best, they vigorously fought for their false perceptions of superiority.

This attitude is even a greater threat today though than 50,000 years ago because Earth population has catapulted from a few hundred thousand to an unbelievable eight billion plus at this writing.

> However, even though the domestication process is vastly limiting, it is not the biggest issue.

The biggest issue: once domesticated, one's Habits continue to self-domesticate.

Self-domestication is actualized by unquestioned Cognitive-Habits, which are left to run without revaluating their purpose or usefulness. After all, Habits are all about maintaining sameness, which as a direct consequence literally blinkers-out options.

By way of example, a quick anecdote follows.

A young girl, Kassie, approaching her sixth birthday is again helping her Mom prepare the bi-monthly family 'get-together' dinner.

Although Kassie has liked being involved with cooking since she was about three, this family event is special to her: both because she loves Pot-Roast, which is always chosen for the occasion and knows that she can have her favorite end piece when she helps.

As usual, she watches her Mom prepare the Pot-Roast to go into a special Cooker. However, this time, as she is a normally inquisitive near-six year old who has observed the tradition for the umpteenth time, Kassie asks her Mom why she cuts off some of the end of the Pot-Roast before putting it into the Cooker.

Kassie's Mom stops her preparation procedures, looks up at the ceiling as if to locate the answer up there, pauses, looks down at the daughter she loves and says, "I don't know … my Mom, your Grandmother, always did that when I helped her and so I do it too".

"I'll tell you what Kassie, its Grandmas turn to have the family get-together dinner next time … let's ask her then, O.K."

The answer was fine for Kassie who said "sure", then returned to joyfully helping her Mom.

Two months went by quickly. Soon, Kassie, her Mom and Dad, and her two twin brothers about three years older arrived at her Grandmas for the family get-together dinner.

As soon as all the hugs were joyfully given Kassie, now six, her Mom and Grandma got busy with preparation.

Chattering away, neither Kassie nor her Mom remembered the 'Pot Roast' conversation until it was time for the Pot-Roast to go into the Cooker. Sure enough, Kassie's Grandma cut a small chunk off its end and then put the remainder into the Cooker.

After quickly telling the story of Kassie's inquiry, Kassie's Mom asked her Mom, Kassie's Grandma, "Why do you cut a chunk off the Pot-Roast before you put it into the Cooker?"

You might have already guessed … Kassie's Grandma's response was identical to that of Kassie's Mom.

Kassie's Grandma stopped her preparation procedures, looked up at the ceiling, paused, looked down at the daughter and granddaughter she loved and said, "I don't know … my Mom, your Grandmother and Kassie's Great-Grandmother always did that when I helped her and so I do it too".

"I'll tell you what Kassie, Grandma said, its Great-Grandmas turn to have the family get-together dinner next time … let's ask her then, O.K."

This idea was fine for both Kassie and her Mom who returned to joyfully helping prepare the feast.

Well you no doubt guessed it again … Two months went by quickly. Soon, Kassie, her Mom and Dad, her two twin brothers and Kassie's Grandma arrived at Kassie's Great-Grandmas for the family get-together dinner. This time though, Kassie's Moms two brothers had arrived for the event with their families in tow from their homesteads in another part of the country.

Great-Grandma, Grandma, Kassie and her Mom soon found themselves busily preparing the meal while chattering away and catching up on all the news.

Sure enough, when Great-Grandma was performing the final preparation for the Pot-Roast to go into the Cooker; she cut a small chunk off its end.

After quickly telling the story of Kassie's inquiry, Kassie's Mom asked her Great-Grandma, "Why do you cut a chunk off the Pot-Roast before you put it into the Cooker?"

"Oh", she said, "during the depression, when we were lucky enough to get a Pot-Roast, which was seldom, we couldn't get a pot big enough to fit it … so we cut a chunk off the end". "Silly habit … don't know why I still do it … force of habit I guess".

When Great-Grandma heard the whole story that her daughter and her daughters-daughter were also cutting off the ends of their Pot Roasts …well let's just say dinner was late as their laughter just wouldn't stop.

Such is the **Habit-Power** that drives each of us: funny sometimes - other times, not so much.

However, when you know **How-We-Work** you are enabled to not only take your **Habit-Power** back and create **pro-habits** with the very same perspicacity, however enhanced to get you what you **TRULY** want but also ignore those **chaos-habit** inhibitors, which are relentlessly holding you in place.

More specifically then, Cognitive-Habits enforce storehoused beliefs and truths by filtering both inbound sensory-fodder (current-new) and recalled or archived-old action-potentials.

> In other words, inbound current-new is filtered by Cognitive-Habits, which provide the **comfort-zone** Experience-Senses, which delude you into accepting sameness or occasional reward as truly living.

Cognitive-Habits by their very nature ensure routine is perceived as acceptable or comfortable and change as taxing and stressful.

Stated differently, Cognitive-Habits control your movements within your Bombardment-Sphere by tailoring Test-Its, which are dually designed to not only avoid UN-recognized and/or higher-intensity but also embrace sameness by moving you away from danger and toward recognized.

> Habits then, like water running down the middle of a flume due to gravity are purposed to keep us in the middle: not up on one side or the other.

In other words, their mandate or 'quiet' imperative is to keep you safe and in the center of your flume. In other words, Cognitive-Habits are 'big-time' risk averse.

> Unfortunately, nothing new ever happens in one's **habit-flume** comfort-zone.

Without question, ongoing self-domestication is the culprit that keeps one from **DO**ing, pursuing, getting and even perceiving what one wants.

However, everyone has another trump card: passion, which equates to knowing what you TRULY want.

Passion Key

Self-limiting Passion and excitement spirits serious repercussions. When not **DO**ing what you want by pursuing your passions, you are grinding at something less, or even much less inspiring for you.

As less inspiring is more like a distasteful chore than a thrill, you **cannot** give it your all.

> Just try to quickly memorize a song you hate vs one you love.

As we now know, when involvement is less than 100%, the **excitement-pillar** that supports both data-archive storehousing (memory) and recall is compromised. Consequently, both storehousing and recall will be limited: sometimes past the point of total malfunction.

> Also, when passion is denied, sensory-acceptance, the core initiator for all data-acquisition, accordingly plummets due to greatly reduced activity.

In other words, due to a lack of enthusiasm, which is the fundamental driver for the way we work, both information capture and recall are restricted, sometimes severely.

> When sensory-acceptance is restricted, then so too are Puzzle creations and consequent population of data-archives limited.

Additionally detrimental when passions are denied is that data-archives are populated with much less action-potential. Resultantly, they will never become the GO-TO's.

Of course, less action-potential also results in recall being compromised as well. In other words, retrieval will be difficult, sketchy and imprecise.

Reduced **fodder** also results in disenfranchising Delving-Trio and Devise-Mulling, which never get to strut-their-stuff because of redundant and/or reduced intensity sensory-fodder (current-new).

Hence, by limiting passion through self-domestication one invariably grinds at, rather than gusto's through their days, months and years: all the while convinced there has to be more to life than this: **AND THERE IS**!

Fortunately, an alternate to the limitation of excitement due to self-domestication is readily available.

Simple Pro-Plan

> Fortuitously, sensory-accepted Deluge 'conditions' delivered to event-horizons can be adjusted: i.e., you can change your environment.

First, recognize that limiting chaos-habits were established through domestication. Next, realize chaos-habits are being sustained by self-domestication. Lastly, seek out vast quantities of **UN**-recognized and intense events.

> By deploying **Pro-Plan**, you start the enjoyable process of creating your own chosen pro-habits.

So whether a trigger temper, addiction or self-sabotaging activities are holding you back, these old domesticated chaos-habits can be usurped with new cherry-picked pro-habits.

Spiriting possible enhancement for improved living-conditions is human ingenuity and adaptability because they enable each person to incorporate many variant Bombardment-Sphere conditions into data-archives.

Thus, by choosing new bombardment, it is possible to select different sensory-input and thereby accumulate the favourable feedback needed to get you what you want.

> In other words, Change your Deluge; upgrade your **L.I.F.E**^{2}.

Think of 'upgrade' this way. In circumstances where sensory-data could be controlled, where it was made continuously 'perfect' and 'precise' (whatever that might be), one could actually determine the content of all data-archives and therefore behaviour, perceptions, thinking, etc.

Unfortunately, such a situation would only create 'brain-clones' restricted in their perception by the very nature of their same accepted sensory-data: Notably, such is brainwashing.

To progress individually and as a species, we do not need same, but different.

Nicely genetics has delivered a broad brush with wide ranges, which provide the capability and capacity to not only accept uncountable finely sliced base frequencies but also combine them in nearly unlimited combinations and permutations.

Combinations are easily demonstrable. Ask ten people to describe a simple object as fully as possible: their accounts will indubitably vary in content and texture.

However, ask their opinion and results will be wildly diverse.

Culture

On a larger scale, one's Culture then is actually definable as a set of accepted, identifiable Cognitive-Habit **living-conditions** handed down by domestication, which folks within a group believe to be best or at least acceptable for their tribes continuation.

Culture can thus be re-defined as groups of tribal Experience-Senses or Cognitive-Habits (beliefs; attitudes; thinking; speaking; etc.), which persist as unquestioned by the majority of its members.

Ways of thinking and speaking are obviously Culture prevalent.

Notably, a slight perceptual difference or tonal (frequency) variance can alert that a newly arrived person does not belong to your tribe. Thus, language and its imperatives establish as keys to identification.

Experience-Sense Pro-Habits

Let's delve into a few of our worst chaos-habits and disclose methodologies to usurp them by creating higher action-potential pro-habits.

Fact: Cognitive-Habits or Experience-Senses are established and powerful.

Our mandate is to create new Experience-Sense pro-habit benefactors and usurp the chaos-habit detractors.

In that myriads of Cognitive-Habits run who we are and perceive ourselves to be, they clearly have substantial power and granularity.

In other words, not only are there lots of them but they also intertwine: i.e., if you pull on one, others with significantly-similar action-potential frequencies will also activate with various degrees of intensity and influence.

Thus, useful would be to have a deep understanding of Experience-Sense origins and their formation process, so establishing new pro-habits can be expedited and not take another lifetime to fashion.

Specifically, *Way Better* Your L.I.F.E^2.: Tactics will focus on three specific Cognitive-Habit categories that have the greatest potential to quickly enhance **L.I.F.E^2.** (Living-in-Full-Experience-and-Excitement) by creating new Way-We-Think pro-habits and relegating the destructive chaos-habit detractors to neural recycling.

Targeted Pro-habit Sets:

1. **Relationships** – with yourself and others
2. **Health** – both physical and mental
3. **Wealth** – joyfulness and material

Relationships: with yourself and others

We end up being us in any case, right? Well, actually not so right.

The relationship with yourself is fundamental: especially **Key** is your self-doubt (Experience-Sense) about your worthiness.

Make no mistake; the self-doubt chaos-habit is both a passion and a positive action **DO**ing killer.

For instance, when you think a new pro-habit is possible and also possible for you, say going for a half-hour walk every day to improve health and resultantly live longer, then a strong possibility exists the new pro-habit will be practiced or be consciously deployed long enough to build its action-potentials to exceed its less desirable lethargy chaos-habit antithesis.

> However, if you don't believe you are worthy due to self-doubt, then passion and therefore activities supporting success will be watered-down in proportion to your **worthiness-barometer**.

Be clear: One's relationship with themselves ultimately determines not only the effectiveness and viability of a new pro-habit but also whether undesirable chaos-habits, which are ever pushing to be utilized, will take over and wreak havoc once again due to their huge action-potentials.

How does a poor self-concept chaos-habit set cause addictions and self-destructive behaviour?

> Brief answer: It keeps you from **DO**ing activities, which facilitate success.

Detailed **Key**: when a poor self-concept chaos-habit is perking away, Devise-Mulling actually not only dispassionately or minimally Solutions Puzzles but also deploys action cancelling **Test-IT**'s.

For better or worse, due to Devise-Mulling's flexible structure, it comes with a debatable chaos-habit bonus: its own invisible, not necessarily friendly inner voice dictator, you know … that negative voice in your head, … normally the harbinger of doom; replete with recriminations and second guessing … **Chatterbox**.

Additionally compromising is that Devise-Mulling's chaos-habit Chatterbox interrupters do not create intense or broad-range Puzzles that would stoke excitement; but instead form only weak **marker-Puzzles** that minimize excitement and therefore action.

> Remember from Book-one that excitement is pivotal to not only establishing larger action-potential deposits within one's data-archives but also enabling copious and easy recall.

It's How-We-Work.

The effect of these Devise-Mulling chaos-habit interrupters typically takes the form of justifications for inaction.

Procrastination chaos-habit, such as I need to relax or I'll get to it later or maybe tomorrow is a main derivative, which provides vagueness instead of excited clarity.

Trust me, when the self-concept chaos-habit is in charge, it is a passion killer.

You may have the best intentions. However, when the self-concept is operating as a chaos-habit, it nullifies your actions.

Resultantly, instead of working and focussing on a project with passion, chaos-habit sponsors non-productive processes for extended periods: like video games, on-line Backgammon, Facebook, etc.

Recollect that Devise-Mulling is one's **only segue** into conscious thought. If Devise-Mulling is compromised, clarity and inspiration are out the window.

Devise-Mulling spirits either clarity when Puzzles are large and Solutioning activity is vigorous due to passion creating copious sensory-accepted feedback-loops; or vagueness and frustration when the opposite is true.

Significantly then, Devise-Mulling engenders two types of outbound **Test-IT**'s (**TI**'s): **vital-TI**'s in response to high-intensity passion, which create broad-scope **DO**ing or Solutioning actions; and **inhibit-TI**'s that dampen appropriate action due to both vague marker-Puzzles and Chatterbox live-feeds into consciousness, which dampen passion and squander cognitive resources.

Private-Self // Public-Self

Let's discover not only how these two Devise-Mulling camps were honed by domestication but also how they come to be habitually sustained and nurtured throughout life.

Once one knows how Devise-Mulling operates, it will be straightforward to harness its power to not only create pro-habits but also push chaos-habits into the neurological recycling bin.

Notably, one's Devise-Mulling complex has the capacity for greater complexity than just one type of devising.

Actually, this multiple-devising capability is what enables everyone's many situational personalities or behavioral ranges: i.e., one is different with a significant other, than with buddies on a Las Vegas trip, than at a stag, than in a boardroom, than while in a stuck dark elevator, etc.

> Excellent actors, without much limitation seem able to tap into and expand this multi-personality capability at will.

Initial Stage

As one is being inundated with others requirements during childhood, most begin to vaguely sense an inner-self/outer-self division exists, which is earmarked by contrast between inner-self wants, hopes and dreams, and outer-self or external expectations of others that pressure you to perform differently you're your natural flow.

Stated differently, one becomes aware behaviour or self-presentation strategies are needed to satisfy the one's **Out-There**; while different wants and needs simultaneously exist for the one **In-Here**.

To accommodate this duality, Cognitive-Habits begin the formation of two bastions: **Public-Self**, which is the outward-facing presentation of oneself to accommodate what one believes is appropriate situational behavior to 'get-by' in the **Out-There**: and **Private-Self**, which is the inward-facing, normally guarded, hidden set of self-value desires and beliefs.

To reconcile the variance, Tier-4 and Tier-5 data-archives start accumulating dichotomous Private-Self and Public-Self (abbreviated as PriS/PubS) Experience-Senses at an early age.

> Without difficulty, Devise-Mulling is normally more than capable of balancing the demands of Out-There self (public) with the desires of the In-Here self (private). Unfortunately, there is a hitch.

Troubles arise when Public-Self is obliged to perform in a way substantially contrary to Private-Self beliefs, wants and/or needs.

When one is unable to fulfill Public-Self requirements to the satisfaction of outer controlling individuals one will probably Experience-Sense stress, dissonance and compounding self-doubt.

When pushed to extreme one can even lose perspective, hope and even consider suicide.

The greater the variance between one's Devise-Mulling Public-Self **Out-There** 'reality' and one's Private-Self's **In-Here** gradients-of-acceptability, the greater the dissonance or tug-of-war between Private-Self and Public-Self.

Finite Energy

Significant dissonance between Private-Self and Public-Self potentially has a serious impact on performance. This is so for two reasons: one's metabolism has finite energy stores; and cognitive-processors have limited capacity.

For clarity, and without consideration for fitness or health levels, let's consider a template scenario where one wakes up in the morning with their particular 100% of available energy.

Important to note is that bio-mechanisms have a very small short-term **energy-battery**.

In other words, Biological energy reserves are small. Therefore, to sustain useful levels of activity, they must be continually replenished by an **optimum** combination of eating and rest.

'Optimum' is highlighted because once the maximum capacity of one's biological energy-battery is reached; no additional food or rest will provide benefit.

Naturally, variable biological and processing demands on energy reserves take their toll throughout the day, even though one's energy-battery may be provided a trickle-charge.

In other words, clear is that a certain percentage of the available energy, which is required for 'normal' ongoing or background maintenance, uses a certain quantity of energy.

Importantly, in a situation where a significant dissonance exists between Private-Self and Public-Self, 70% to 90% of available opening energy reserves could be being diverted and thus utilized for non-useful chaos-habit Devise-Mulling activities: such as, Chatterbox as it administers self-doubt and inhibit-TIs.

> If you have ever experienced your Chatterbox endlessly mulling options that have minimal clarity or resolution possibility, then you comprehend the extent of energy-battery drain first-hand.

Problem is this leaves available only 10% to 30% of the opening energy for fluctuating daily demands. This is a significant problem in logistics for our bio-selves because to usefully and effectively Solution, mechanisms need 80%.
This is a substantial and devastating shortfall in terms of creating anything new.

> No wonder when the Chatterbox is jabbering away and consequently compromising your energy reserves, you feel drained and unable to manage.

In addition, no wonder one can feel life is overwhelming, as you feel unable to get what you **TRULY** want when everything seems hard and/or impossible due energy reserves being drained by chaos-habits.

Rectification

So, how does one avoid or remedy PriS/PubS conflict conditions, which are contributing to duress and energy-battery drain?

Succinct answer: Adjust physical position and/or activity as radically as necessary to flourish a substantially different Bombardment-Sphere environment that is exciting.
This strategy of course works because it changes sensory-accepted events and Puzzles and Test-Its and therefore perspective and attitudes.

Stated differently, remove yourself from the situation or physical environment and **DO** something intensely different.

> As one intuitively (a Devise-Mulling competency) knows to 'step out for a breath of fresh air' in stressful situations: **DO** that.

Rectification of dissonance or PriS/PubS conflict begins with adjusting the impacts on sensory event-horizons by cutting out the disrupting Deluge source.

In other words, dissonance can be extinguished (at least temporarily) by the alteration of one's Bombardment-Sphere positioning or more accurately the amendment to something exciting of the thorny sensory-accepted Deluge events proliferating within one's Bombardment-Sphere.

> It is by improvement of initializing action-potentials, which ultimately manifest as different Cognitive-Habit attitudes and behaviors (as a consequence of being subsequently processed by various mechanisms) that provides THE substantial clue to alleviating dissonance, conserving one's energy-battery and thereby enhancing one's living-conditions and living-experiences.

Now the Cognitive-Habit and Devise-Mulling mechanics of this aspect of **How-We-Work** are understood, let's move forward.

Alignment

When one learns how to productively engage Devise-Mulling at will, one can consciously create Puzzles and deploy improved Solutions by understanding that betterment of attitudes and perceptions is vastly dependent on how much you **DO** to create more-useful sensory-accepted events.

> In other words, knowledge of **How-We-Work** can be utilized to not only engage the most-useful actions, thereby choicefully adjusting one's living-experience, but also maintain both integration and integrity of one's **PriS//PubS** camps; and resultantly minimize self-doubt, dissonance, energy drain and maximize passion.

Thus, in the relationship with yourself and others, it is critical to ensure Private-Self and Public-Self are closely aligned and do not significantly conflict.

Pretending or not being true to your Private-Self desires and passions simply takes too much energy.

When Private-Self is not closely aligned, it will be metabolically impossible to energy-battery support a Public-Self persona and remain productive and/or rational.

Furthermore, when you don't get what your Private-Self **TRULY** wants and needs, pro-habit excitement and passion will not happen either: but the chaos-habits of sadness, self-doubt, depression, anger, etc. most definitely will.

As you are progressing on your journey to more closely integrate Private-Self and Public-Self ensure that you do not beat yourself up for who you aren't yet: Instead, celebrate who you are now.

In other words, rather than disenfranchising yourself for what you have not yet accomplished, focus instead on what you have accomplished: even if in beginning stages achievements seem, from your Chatterbox chaos-habit perspective, more valuable to others than to yourself.

Celebration works because exercising this **Key** element intensifies current events,

   which in turn makes them more exciting,
     which creates greater action-potentials and thus fodder,
       which creates copious dynamic Puzzles,
         which engages Cognition-Complex,
           which in turn enables significantly more neural-pathway connections,
             which more expansively populate data-archives,

  which in turn creates Test-Its that expand possibilities by
     'shedding-light' (sensory-acceptance) where there was once
     darkness (underpopulated data-archives).

Pro-habit Interrupters

So, what is going to get in your pro-habit creation way?

When **DO**ing does not go according to plan to get you what you want, there are five possible limiting culprits.

1. Insufficient intensity: this will result in either not engaging Cognition-Complex and/or creating minimalistic marker-Puzzles.

2. Inadequate continual new sensory fodder: fodder is needed to provide the 'answers' (F-Puzzles) for effective Solutioning.

3. Chaos-habit Chatterbox: it causes Devise-Mulling to create crushing inhibit-TIs.

4. Obstructive Experience-Senses (Cognitive-Habits) with huge action potentials: Devise-Mulling will incorporate these and thus filter-out Test-Its by

downgrading **Cognition-Complex** intensity. This action will also ensure that not only will Cognition-Complex not be alerted but also Test-Its required for feedback be nullified.

5. Insufficiently populated data-archives: limiting useful comparative processing, these will either not have applicable frequency reserves or be minimal.

'Get in Your Way' Rectification

Insufficient Intensity

This one is fairly straightforward to resolve: just throw yourself 100% or whole-heartedly into whatever 'project' you choose. Travel in the evolving directions with pro-habit passion.

However, if having difficulty mustering the passion or excitement due to contradictory chaos-habits joining in the 'holding-you-back' fight, like procrastination or Chatterbox telling you it won't make a difference, then solicit help. After all, everyone needs inspiration from external sources from time to time.

For instance, if your chaos-habit is being a couch potato then allow others to help by going for fitness-walks with you. Have them choose an interesting topic of conversation for each walk. To ramp up the fun gradient wear some way-out-there garb; walk backwards and sideways; skip; whatever it takes.

Remember though, if you don't break a sweat then you are not walking but sauntering and sauntering is NOT going to improve your health because you have not exceeded your biological activity threshold.

In other words, if you are heading toward creating a fitness pro-habit set make sure you walk fast enough to return home a little damp: otherwise minimal metabolic effect yields ... you guessed it ... minimal physical improvement.

Truism: Don't expect to get more out of a 'System' than you put in. In other words, do not expect 100% out when you only put 30% effort in.

If you are having a hard time **DO**ing for yourself how about **DO**ing with a significant other or create an entire support team to help you accomplish your new pro-habit: most have the same issues, so will be very receptive.

This cooperative tack will also fit nicely into creating the pro-habit of building stronger and more fulfilling relationships with yourself and whomever else.
If friends are scarce due to their chaos-habits, schedules or whatever, join a walking group. Be assured that **DO**ing will stir your Bombardment-Sphere.

Result: all sorts of fun opportunities and options will pop-up, Puzzles will be created, and thus excitement increase.

> Alternately, create a more useful fitness pro-habit set so your kids and loved ones can enjoy your healthy company longer.

Inadequate Sensory Fodder

This one is also straightforward to solve, although potentially more difficult, because it requires you get **Out-There** and **DO** more activities. Of course, one can be your walking group: by the way, keep searching until you find one that creates excitement for you.

Not surprisingly, little new sensory-fodder is provided in familiar surroundings: like sitting on the couch and watching T.V. All the new exciting stuff is **Out-There** already perking: all you have to **DO** is get yourself inserted into the activity stream to create an Enjoy pro-habit.

Be aware Chatterbox and the Habit-Duo really do not like change: This is a fact you have learned from this book series. They are designed to drive you through your day by **approaching familiar** while **avoiding UN-familiar**: This of course is one's comfort-zone.

Trust me … NOTHING new ever happens in your comfort-zone: so get out of it and grab some excitement, build experiences and Puzzles, then enjoy Figuring-It-Out.

The rewards will be enormous once you are successful at telling your domesticated Chatterbox chaos-habit to shut-up and stop holding you in place.

Chatterbox Chaos-Habit

I know I have touched on the insidious Chatterbox chaos-habit before but it really, really needs to be replaced by its pro-habit benefactor counterpart: **Support-bot**.

Remember our discussions regarding Finite-Energy, and Private-Self//Public-Self and its origins in domestication?

Without taking control of this Chatterbox chaos-habit passion-killer almost everything you engage in will seem exhausting and overwhelming.

This is because Chatterbox will not only drain and waste huge quantities of your daily Devise-Mulling energy stores (maybe upwards of 80%) but also thus stop you from making decisions about or even recognizing what would be beneficial for you.

Chatterbox has existed and evolved since you were young and thus become a powerful Experience-Sense.

Chatterbox has had decades of action-potentials added to its Tier-5 arsenals. Therefore, so Support-bot will become the *GO-TO* benefactor instead, one needs to be extremely passionate while building Chatterboxes pro-habit nemesis.

Start by **DO**ing the following: Every time Chatterbox chaos-habit pipes up, the best course of action is to extremely loudly (even if its only in your head) tell it to shut-up and go away. Be as rude as you like: it really helps!

This strong assertive stance works for two reasons.

Part of the Support-bot pro-habit set is recognizing Chatterbox as detrimental to getting what you TRULY want. Fortunately, as Support-bot is new and has no counterpart, it does not require huge action-potential to activate it.

Secondly, passionately telling Chatterbox to shut-up (intensely) will engage Cognition-Complex's' Devise-Mulling and Delving-Trio.

Once engaged will not only Devise-Mulling create Puzzles, which it will Solution by sending copious **Test-IT**s outbound for feedback but also Delving-Trio fire their specific brands of various intensity Test-Its.

Thus, passionate refusal to allow Chatterbox to rule your thoughts will provide enormous action-potential fodder to populate your fledgling pro-habit Support-bot Experience-Sense benefactor instead. Thereby, Support-bot will quickly become the GO-TO instead and thus enable rather than disable your hopes and dreams.

In other words, each time you passionately deny credibility to and interaction with Chatterbox chaos-habit, your new Support-bot pro-habit will gain strength (more action-potential) until it and you are in charge instead.
This is How-We-Work. Give it a try: this really, really works.

Once in charge, the Support-bot pro-habit via Devise-Mulling will be feeding you possibilities instead of dampening you with limitations.

Of course, possibilities will launch you into an ever-expanding world of passion and excitement, and eliminate the feelings of hopelessness and desolation that were so freely provided by the Chatterbox chaos-habit debilitator.

Obstructive Experience-Senses

Experience-Senses or Cognitive Habits are Tier-5 data-archives. As such, by the time we have acquired language skills they are already driving beliefs, preferences, attitudes, etc. by mixing current-new with Cognitive habitual assumptions.

> Experience-Senses are supported by large action-potentials and are therefore the premier **GO-TO** Cognitive-Habit interface that Devise-Mulling utilizes to rapidly respond when comparing **current-new** to **archived-old**.

As we now know, complex Puzzle groups (like learning how to fly a plane) take longer to solve than simpler ones (like bike riding) because many (thousands) Test-It cycles are necessary for Cognition-Complex to gather answers (F-Puzzles) via cyclical sensory-feedback from the Out-There.

Experience-Senses loosely parallel Body-Self habitual responders in regards to rapid response-action recommendations. Consequently, Mind-Self regularly employs Cognitive-Habits, which utilize Test-Its to suggest rapid **first-blush** action-responses and effect outbound assumptions.

In other words, when UN-recognized and/or sufficiently high intensity events Bombard sensory event-horizons and thus instigate Cognitive-Alerts, both Cognition-

Complex's Ranged-Delving and Devise-Mulling (by frequency matching amalgamated current-new to Cognitive-Habit archived-old) issue first-responder **TEST**-its and **Test-IT**s (respectively), initially devised from Experience-Senses, as their first line of rapid defense to keep you safe.

Like most things in our Universe-H, Experience-Senses or Cognitive-Habits are also double-edged swords: i.e., they can be useful or detrimental. For example, the Sun provides warmth but can also burn.

For instance, one useful Cognitive-Habit is a 'Pause' pro-habit (set) that allows a **time-space** between unfolding events and response to them.
In other words, more useful would be to allow time-space for evaluation, by consciously commissioning Devise-Mulling to Figure-It-Out by creating E-Puzzles (questioning) and seeking answers (F-Puzzles) by **DO**ing (investigating via feedback).

In *Way Better* Your L.I.F.E^2. terms, provide time for Devise-Mulling to create Puzzles, send **Test-It**s, gather feedback (answer Puzzles) and deploy best-practices responses. In other words, rather than allowing cognitive chaos-habits to rule you, take back your Habit-Power and choose to create pro-habit actions.

Less useful is where the 'Assumptive' chaos-habit is the **GO-TO** instead. Unlike its 'Pause' pro-habit, it will result in angry, erratic, destructive and biased outbursts that align poorly to the ongoing situation.

To underline the point, here is a scenario where two people are talking. Ideally, in a two person conversational scenario, even though the two rolls flip-flop, one will be the **Sender** and the other the **Receiver** throughout the exchange.

To audio sensors (ears), speech is delivered as a sequential stream of noise.

This means that when the Sender requires 50 words to present their full viewpoint, the words will follow one after the other. Obviously, if the Sender is interrupted by the Receiver after 15 words, then the Senders viewpoint could not have been fully understood.

Interruption or **Talk-Over** is usually interpreted by others as unfavourable. In the 'Talk-over' scenario the Receiver is powerless to discriminate between conversation types from low information banter or chatter to high information listening. In other words, most know a gradient of interaction modes exist for different conversational scenarios: some O.K. for talk over; others not.

No doubt during interruption the 'Talk-Over' chaos-habit is being rapidly triggered as the sensory-information data-stream is arriving (i.e., as in hearing the Senders first 15 words).

In *Way Better* Your L.I.F.E^2.: Tactics terms, how does the triggering function work?

Firstly, the Receivers 'Talk-Over' chaos-habit is triggered by **current-new**. Recall, due to self-domestication that endorses such behaviour as acceptable, high action-potential significantly-similar Cognitive-Habits become collaborative GO-TO's as well.
Secondly, Cognition-Complex is activated because both the **UN**-recognized and higher-intensity requirements are satisfied. In other words, where the topic has new content and is provocative to the Receiver, intensity will be higher.

In this circumstance, Devise-Mulling will kick-in and invoke significantly-similar Experience-Senses, which thus engage the high action-potential GO-TO 'Talk-Over' chaos-habit. Thus involved, Devise-Mulling loads its **Test-ITs** with applicably biased 'Talk-Over' chaos-habit action-potentials; not current-new.

Thus, when Devise-Mulling **Test-ITs** hit Template-Component they are loaded with recognized fodder. Therefore, Template-Component makes its recommendation to Response-Component from its previously Patterned data-archive, rather than from newly formed configurations.

Response-Component, also recognizing content, engages neural-pathways and hormonal responses to fulfill the recommended Patterns. Result is Body-Self movements, which include body-adjustments, such as facial expressions and voice activation or interruption.

Insufficiently Populated Data-archives

Without **DO**ing, consequential data-archive population is severely limited. When deficit is the case, one will perform all kinds of erroneous behaviors or auto-responses. Conversely, with sufficient **DO**ing anything is possible.

'Pygmalion' by George Bernard Shaw provides a great example of data-archive deficit and the passion-power we all have to recognize, overcome it and trust in ourselves.

Obstructive chaos-habit Experience-Senses abound with Pickering and Higgins. Pickering is so biased that he wagers Higgins cannot take such a "ragamuffin" (Eliza) and have her speak and behave like a Duchess.

> In other words, Pickering believes (obstructive chaos-habit) that Eliza has neither the neural capacity nor the processing capability to populate the data-archives necessary to emulate a Duchesses behavior.

Eliza certainly had the passion to speak 'properly'. Her motivation was the belief that when she could **DO** that, she could get a position in a flower shop. Although motivating for her at the time (due to her insufficiently populated data-archives), she came to realize a vast other world existed **Out-There**.

Although her Public-Self was stereotyped by others as worthless, Eliza not only believed in herself but also had no doubt she could become part of something much bigger and more important.

> Stated in **Tactics** terms, Eliza was confident she could create more-useful pro-habits (thinking and speech) and usurp non-useful limiting chaos-habits like Chatterbox.

Just like Eliza, everyone's Devise-Muller can choose what he or she TRULY wants, create inception E-Puzzles and then flat-out go for it by **DO**ing.

Eliza was also smart to understand she needed to solicit help to get her what she **TRULY** wanted. Eliza never took no for an answer but pushed her **DO**ing to the max. Although not all her efforts were successful, she stuck with her dream. Her passion made the difference because as we now know, excitement is the underpinning of both rapid data-archive population (memory) and pertinent detailed recall: both necessary to get what you TRULY want.

You can be confident that if you are not getting what you want one or both of two reasons are the culprit: You are not passionate enough to make your dream a 'TRULY want' and/or you do not sufficiently believe in your capabilities to 100% engage.

If either chaos-habit above has truth for you (ho-hum and/or self-doubt), the consequence will be that you are not getting what you TRULY want because you are not stoking your passions with zeal.

The upshot is that the debilitating self-doubt chaos-habit set is in charge, corrupting current-new with dysfunctional disenfranchising archived-old Cognitive-Habits.

Bottom line: if you are having difficulty shaking addiction chaos-habits that are not serving you, have passion for whatever processes you are employing or **DO**ing to create new pro-habits.

Not everything you **DO** will be ultimately 100% immediately (or short-term) useful: but, to sufficiently populate data-archives, all the **DO**ing sidebars need to be done with passion.

Get help with your **DO**ing by those who have experience and a genuine commitment to assisting because their pro-habits will gradually populate yours as well.
Such is the true symmetry of group dynamics: each provides excitement, attitude and perspective to get what the group TRULY wants; and therefore you get what you TRULY want as well. What could be better, really!

Group Dynamics

Speaking of groups, let's deal with a group that has been prevalent or at least accepted as a societal norm for many millennia - at least in the view of the vast majority. Few probably think of two people, committed as a 'couple' being a group but explanations below will ratify that it most definitely is.

The **couple-group** gets its 'modern-day' (last 3 millennia give or take) spin from both Religious and Political doctrines, which were specifically contrived to ensure elitist control and power over property ownership and country boundaries.

As origins are rarely questioned, the concept of couple, significant-other or dedication to one other as a mate has become accepted as customary on this world: I am not suggesting this is a 'bad' thing.

Understandably, 'customary' encapsulates culturally diverse norms whose beliefs have been sustained by millennia of domestication. As beliefs are Experience-Senses with five Tiers of data-archives, which have been domesticated since birth, these GO-TO Cognitive-Habits are seldom to never questioned.

Even if cultural standards are questioned, pressure exerted by ones family, friends, clergy and acquaintances soon either quashes alternate thinking and/or sets up dissonance between ones Private-Self and Public-Self. Resultantly, one stays 'in the closet' so-to-speak feeling disturbed that not only is their thinking flawed but also they are also somehow broken.

Dissonance is a huge issue because without an aligned Private-Self (PriS) and Public-Self (PubS) – i.e., where they are very close to being one and the same - one just can't be right for somebody else.

This is because when you get seriously involved with one other person the complexity escalates from **two to 10** relationships as detailed below: no wonder couple-relationships can be so difficult, when one is unaware of all the interactions.

Couples-Relationship Decagon

Please note: The 'Him' and 'Her' below (and derivatives) are used for clarity only and in no way intended to exclude alternate love relationships.

In this authors view, wherever there is love, caring and respect, life is good.

- **Him to Himself**
    - His PriS:
        1) his private belief in his value or worth
    - His PubS:
        2) how he views his own value and worth to the external-world
- **Him to Partner**
    - His valuation of her PriS:
        3) his evaluation of her self-concept
    - His appraisal of her PubS:
        4) his appreciation, respect or dislike of her PubS behaviour
- **His Couple View**
        5) How he views them functioning as a couple both privately and publicly

----

- **Her to Herself**
    - Her PriS:
        6) how she views her own value and worth in her private-world
    - Her PubS:
        7) how she views her own value and worth in the external-world
- **Her to Partner**
    - Her view of his PriS:
        8) her evaluation of his self-concept
    - Her view of his PubS:
        9) her appreciation, respect or dislike of his PubS behaviour
    - **Her Couple View**
        10)   How she views them functioning as a couple both privately and publicly

Here is where I am going with this. As we know, the consequence of not knowing either How-We-Work or how an 'anything' works will only spirit conjecture, which is imprecise and flawed by its very nature.

As guessing only spirits trial-and-error vagueness, not clarity, one can confidently conclude this as a non-useful strategy for creating a joyful and fulfilling couple or Private-Self relationship. At best, the trial-and-error approach will both seriously degrade your Partners trust and confidence Experience-Senses of you and engender frustration and upset.

However, once the Relationship-Decagons interpersonal implications are understood, you and your Partner will both be enabled to clearly appreciate the others perspectives.

In other words, relating to your Partner will cease to be 'best-guess'. Instead, both of you will be enabled to not only accelerate intimacy but also awesome your lives together.

Couples Interaction Pivots

Your relationship with yourself is of paramount importance because your Experience-Senses of YOU are the primary **expectation-filters** for all your endeavors (or avoidances). Remember, this is because one's granular Cognitive-Habits run most (upwards of 95%) of one's day.

Make no mistake your self-doubt (Experience-Sense) chaos-habit has placed you on your **private-world** worthiness-gradient. Self-placement is critical to understand because a direct correlation exists between your self-determined worthiness-gradient position and your ability to be aware of and/or get what you (and/or your Partner) TRULY want in the **external-world**.

When Private-Self does not consider itself worthy, competent or capable, even though that may be an utterly erroneous conclusion to an 'onlooker', chaos-habits (engaging automatically on your behalf) will drive actions that will be polar-opposite to the choices that would have been made, if you felt worthiness pro-habit empowered.

Negative self-perception is a critical driver in couple-relationships (and other types as well) because chaos-habits will power you to accept only that which is recognized or 'comfortable': such is **Habit-Force**.

Recognition of Habit-Power is important because the 'normal' actions one takes are seldom out of one's habit-enforced comfort zones … unless … one inserts two ingredients: huge excitement and a fresh Bombardment-Sphere.

Beware! Nothing new or exciting ever happens in the 'comfort-zone'.

Fulfilling relationships are enhanced by plenty and damaged or dismantled by scarcity.

Remember, no way a half-full bucket has enough reserve to fill another empty bucket of the same size.

In other words, one cannot feel badly enough about themselves to make any relationship better.

Remember, those bothersome self-doubt chaos-habits are always on the prowl severely limiting your appreciation of you.

Self-doubt actually skews the way one perceives the world, so that one may not clearly 'see' or hear impacting events. It will always bias perception away from positive **DO**ing that is critical to enable the fulfillment of your passion, purpose and greatness.

Always providing a negative spin, self-doubt chaos-habit keeps you in the center of the water flume. Thus, it impedes full actualization of your true capability, competence and confidence.

In *Way Better* Your L.I.F.E^2. terms, activity obstruction occurs because when current-new is incorporated with the action-potential of the self-doubt chaos-habit Experience-Sense, the resulting outbound Test-Its actually curtail excitement rather than spiriting involved activity.

Limiting occurs because Cognition-Complex, which as we know is the arena that supplies the outbound Test-Its for involved possibly conscious activity, simply does not get engaged.

Subsequently and even more detrimental, the reduction in dynamic Test-Its reduce sensory-feedback, which further reduces excitement and involvement. One would no doubt call this a downward activity spiral.

　　　The self-doubt yo-yo is however escapable: **DO** your passions.

Don't let anybody, especially self-doubt and Chatterbox chaos-habits, put you down or slow you down: get **DO**ing!

Absolutely, **Passion-experiences** will make the excitement pro-habit the **GO-TO** instead: give it a try (yes, it's a dare!).

Consequently, will not only your private and public selves become ever more contiguous but so too will your self-doubt chaos-habit continue to be usurped by the confidence pro-habit.

Additionally, your Partner, as well as others within your sphere of influence will rally to your side thereby accelerating your excitement and fulfillment even more.

The positive effect on your Partner will also be astounding. Excitement is contagious because does it not only positively change your Bombardment-Sphere but your significant others as well.

　　　One's Bombardment-Sphere is such a significant factor because when you positively change your Bombardment-Sphere you immediately begin to *Way Better* Your L.I.F.E^2.

Experience-Sense Controllers

When one encounters any situation where experience is minimal, both unfamiliar and uncomfortable sensations will manifest; sometimes to the point of feeling as if you are dreaming or 'out of your element'.

Of course, we now understand that the synonymous with 'feelings' perpetrator is Experience-Senses. Recall that Experience-Senses show up as they do, due in large part to an influx of either current-new and/or Devise-Mullings Puzzle-solving activities (either silent or with some gradient of awareness) creating (appropriate to Puzzles and/or Deluge intensity) Test-Its.

In this type of situation Experience-Senses so render because when the action-potentials of frequency appropriate data-archives for current-new Deluge are scarce, Devise-Mulling cannot retrieve sufficient frequency applicable archived-old to immediately Solution its newly created Puzzles.

Consequently, Devise-Mulling goes for significantly-similar. It is because these retrieved frequencies can be so radically different from current-new that one has the sense of being 'out-of-sync' with 'reality'.

Compounding the effect is the **Movie-Of-Your-Life** presentation center. In such circumstances, it struggles to maintain a continuous presentation stream. Resultantly it is impelled to accesses significantly-similar data-archives.

However, in brand-new situations action-potential retrieval can be a far cry from current-new frequencies. In other words, when significant disconnects of this type occur, presentation is composed of mostly irrelevant 'fill' derived from closest frequency-similar data-archives. When inexperienced, 'fill' can be vastly different than current-new events, which results in one 'feeling' compromised.

Further exacerbating ones situational-senses (as a consequence of the frequency-dissimilarity between current-new and retrieved archived-old) are not only Experience-Senses but also Test-Its similarly compromised.

When interpreted and deployed by Body-Self (or Soma-Self) these conflicted Test-Its can impel a broad range of mot-so-useful hormonal and physical outcomes.

Potential responses to unfamiliar Bombardment-Sphere event strings, probably familiar to most can include chaotic actions, quivering, sweating, itching, blurred vision, light-headedness, passing-out, rapid heartbeat, speech impediment, flight-or-flight response and so on.

Strong parallels to the above exist as well when you first meet someone. The situation feels new because you have minimal data-archives or Experience-Senses regarding them. 'Vagueness' and unfamiliar excitement both manifest because insufficient experience with that person has yet neither populated Mind-Self's five data-archive Tiers nor engaged Puzzle Solutioning.

In other words, in relation to the copious new frequencies bombarding your sensory-receptors, because of this person being in your physical proximity (in your Bombardment-Sphere), Cognitive-Habits are currently minimal.

Introduction

What

What is Attraction?

Before I answer this age-old poser, a little background refresher is in order to ensure applicable concepts are in place.

Universe-H provisions everything, without exception. In other words, Universe-H supplies both the fundamental energy building blocks and the physical laws that fastidiously dictate operating parameters. This is true of not only energy itself but also the 'allowable' interactions of energy building blocks, which amass into ever-larger physical constructs or 'matter'.

> **Energy** is not one thing.

Instead, the twelve or so **Base-one** energy-signatures (BOES) each persist within their own particular frequency range, which cumulatively, without gap, comprise the entire gamut of the Electromagnetic Frequency Spectrum (EFS).Thus, BOES form the foundation for all more complex Universe-H constructs.

> To restate, if we had the correct tools, **Base-one** energy-signatures could be confirmed as the continuous end-to-end underpinning of the entire Electromagnetic Frequency Spectrum (EFS). As such, BOES are the consistent and immutable baseplate for Universe-H laws, energy types and energy accumulations Such as **Base-two** QUARKS that form mass.

For those who have ever played with the larger Lego offerings, think of the provided mat as the Base-one foundation upon which everything else that is built on top relies for its fit, extents and unchanging support.

The Electromagnetic Frequency Spectrum discloses two Universe-H truths. First, everything in Universe-H is reliant on the stability or SAMENESS of Base-One energy-signatures.

Thus, as we work our way up the scale from infinitesimal to larger, it is actually the Base-One substrate that, by variously interacting (without losing individual frequency identities) creates the fundamental **Base-three** 'mass' particles called Protons, Neutrons and Electrons.

Base-three constructs in turn are the building blocks of matter (mass actually) whose various combinations and permutations also vibrate slightly differently one-from-the-next: as do their 'energy' parents.

Due to their stable properties as determined by Universe-H allowable parameters or Laws these Base-three particles not only group together but also variously interact to form the ranges of matter that we call elements, which are **Base-four** constructs.

> Consequently, in that we are contained within Universe-H and therefore must abide by its laws, the fundamental determiner of How-We-Work is the immutability of Base-One frequencies that define all energy and mass in our vast Cosmos home.

Significant for discussions then, is that each coalesced Base-four 'mass-bit' also stringently presents only its unique and immutable frequency and therefore vibrates in its own very specific and immutably the SAME way.

So, as we climb the rungs from Base-One to our **Base-eight** formulation as a human biological entity, lots of ever larger amalgamations have occurred: molecules (Base-four), compounds (Base-five), cells (Base-Six) and tissues (Base-Seven). Keep in mind due to various complexities, there are sub-categories of each Base level as well.

At each **Base-level**, two absolutes are notable. First, each of the lower Base-level building blocks never forfeit their frequency identity. This is immutably so, even though the frequency outcome of their collaborative dance with other Base-levels results in a frequency different than any one of its members.

A simple example will explain better. Intriguingly, Water is composed of two gasses: specifically two Hydrogen atoms and one Oxygen atom. Even though they are neither the same size nor the same vibration, the three Base-three particles dance together forming a new compound.

> The new 'water' amalgamation not only has completely different properties than its Base-three members but also uniquely and reliably vibrates differently from each of its component parts. In other words, they do not 'mush' together and lose their Base-three level frequency identities.

Universe-H's **Law of Coalescence of Energy** works as follows: immutable BOES form relationships with compatible BOES to form larger Base-two constructs, which in turn form collaborative interactions (NOT mushing) with other compatible Base-Two constructs to form larger Base-Three amalgamations: and so on.

Stated differently for clarity, it is phenomenal that even though various Base cooperatives dance to produce both new physical attributes (properties) and different frequencies and thus vibrations, the vibrational properties of the lower-rung Base-level building blocks never mush together but instead remain immutably discrete.

> Thus, the Base-one immutable-frequency property is what enables separation and therefore all the amazing and substantial recycling and remixing possibilities.

Unique vibration is also true for the human construct as well. In other words, Humans also present a holistic vibration within a narrow range on the Electromagnetic Frequency Spectrum.

> One's vibration is comprised not only of all one's biological material but also the sum-total of action-potentials that have been morphed into fodder and stored in data-archives, which represents the sum-total of one's experiences.

The first portion of the answer to the 'attraction' puzzle then is that, even though composed of uncountable Base-three through Base-seven components, each person also, due to the quantity of contained components – because of one's physical size - vibrate differently, even though only very slightly, one person to the next.

The second portion necessary to Solution the 'attraction' Puzzle, hinted at above is actually storehoused within one's data-archives. Specifically, the second contributor to a person's vibration is storehoused Body-Self and Mind-Self fodder or experiences.

> Remember, fodder is actually the culmination of all one's sensory-accepted events or experiences.

Recall, action-potential is not just one thing either. Like everything else in Universe-H, action-potentials also present within a range.

Even though the instigator for action-potential is mechanical or impact energy, it is the mandate of each sensory-array to first convert the mechanical energy to electrical energy and then apply its own twist, which results in a unique action-potential signature.

In other words, each impact location or sensory-array handles the conversion (mechanical to electrical) slightly differently. Sensory-arrays spin each location-specific sensory-event slightly differently, which results in its action-potentials having their own range-of-frequencies.

> In other words, each manifestation as fodder also has a distinct frequency-signature, which is the neurophysiological currency one relies on to recall and compare current-new to archived-old.

The upshot of the above review is to point-out that each person biologically vibrates slightly differently within a narrow range, due to three vibrational modulators: genetics, which provides one's physical parameters; your environment and habits, which contribute to one's body size and shape; and experiences, which storehouse experiences as fodder.

> Thus, one vibrates differently as they physically grow and acquire experiences: i.e., your baby self vibrated very differently than your grown self now does.

Perhaps an infant's lack of cerebral action-potential is the reason most love babies: i.e., their vibration is almost pure genetics at birth.

Now the review is complete, the point is that both your Body-Self and your Mind-Self contribute to one's overall vibration. Thus, your Self-Duo vibrates and the person you meet presents their Self-Duo vibration.

Just as certain frequency combinations are incompatible at each Base-level within Universe-H, so are certain peoples Self-Duo's (Body-Self and Mind-Self) frequency combinations incompatible.

> For instance, no way Helium and oxygen are sufficiently frequency compatible to form a compound; even though Helium's atomically adjacent to its Hydrogen precursor that forms water.

In other words, if one person's Body-Self is vibrating at the one-inch mark (using a ruler as a convenient measure) and the other at the eleven-inch mark, the overlap necessary for **immediate** attraction will probably be missing. However, if one person's Body-Self vibrates on five and the other on five and a half, a strong overlap and therefore possible attraction could result.

Original vibrational assessment is handled by the Body-Self's primary brain: Recall it is a rapid survival assessment. You might also recall it operates in the millisecond-by-millisecond world, where it assesses survival potential based on Deluge events being **UN**-recognized and/or higher-intensity: like meeting someone for the first time.

In less than 30 milliseconds, the Body-Self's assessment is typically complete.

However, due to **UN**-recognized and/or higher-intensity conditions of just meeting someone, a Cognitive-Alert is issued. Thus, Mind-Self gets involved and not only assess the Body-Self delivered Cognitive-Alert packet but also brings Visual-sensors on-line.

Additionally, Figure-It-Out deploys Experience-Senses (Cognitive-Habits). This aspect is important because Mind-Self has **habitual** ranges-of-acceptability (ROA's), which introduce attenuated vibrations to the 'processing cauldron': i.e., attributes you like and those you don't: like fat is OK, or not; tall is OK, or not; long hair on a guy is OK, or not; voice, etc., etc.

Resultantly, Mind-Self provides deeper assessment based on the other person's self-presentation. Importantly at this stage, when comparative-analysis on Cognitive-Pathway Three or Four evaluate much current-new to be outside one's many ROA's (Ranges-of-Acceptability), attraction will not happen either.

> Often one hears something like: When I first saw the person, I wasn't interested, but when I talked with them, I was completely excited by who they were. Vice versa also occurs: he/she is so good looking but their personality is a downer.

Note in both cases, Body-Self assessment is first and Mind-Self's second: This order is a Key to the way we roll.

To round out 'attraction' discussions, let's take a different approach.

When you interact with someone for the first time, whether in person, over the phone or see them from a distance you get an almost immediate Body-Self assessment impression.

How does it work that one's **attraction-gradient** rapidly yields a sense from appeal-to-repulsion? Not only this, most times they are eerily accurate.

So, let's delve into what drives this rapid assessment?

Firstly, the 'spontaneous' feelings you experience are in place as part of survival strategy, whose origins are traceable to genetic (DNA) blueprints. The genetically mechanisms responsible for such 'instant' responses are integrated into both Body-Self and Mind-Self (the Self-Duo) and encompass sensory-arrays, neural data-archives and processing capacities.

Recall both Soma-Sensors and Cognitive-Sensors (vision) deal with Deluge in a millisecond-by-millisecond timeframe: actually, as stated in the first two books in about three millisecond chunks or 'snippets'.

However, Cognitive-Self's Cognition-Complex, which only activates when Cognitive-Alert delivers a data-package (due to action-potential being **UN**-recognized and/or higher-intensity), operates in a second-by-second timeframe. This means that Body-Self millisecond timeframes are imperceptible to Mind-Self's Cognitive processors.

> Thus, as a first contact with someone fulfills the **UN**-recognized (and probably the higher-intensity) requirement will not only Cognitive-Alerts be issued and escalation to at least Cognitive-Pathway three but also intensity will be additionally incremented due to remarkable-feature assessment by Visual-Works.

Also though, depending on the circumstances of the encounter, casual, anticipatory or at gunpoint, the Cognitive-Alert tailoring will be quite different.

In other words, the Cognitive-Alert will be either a **request-alert** when the meet-up is non-life-threatening … or an **imperative-alert** when **Threat-Check** determines unfolding events as **significantly-intense**.

Therefore, after the brief restatement above, here is the point: Attraction and detraction are traceable to both genetic and sensory origins.

Both are therefore a direct consequence of the tens-of-thousands of rapidly occurring millisecond **micro-events** that are recognizable to Body-Self's neural processors but cannot be recognized by Cognitive-Self because it is simply not designed to relate to the minutia of millisecond timeframes.

Proving this claim is fairly easy. Put a newscast on pause, then advance it one frame at a time. Notice the multitudes of transitional **micro-variances** in facial and body expressions that we simply do not cognitively 'see' or discriminate at higher 'speeds'. The micro-events are however captured by sensory-arrays then assessed and evaluated by applicable Body-Self processors.

It is during the Cognitive-Alert and visual-sensor integration processing stages where Cognition-Complex's Devise-Mulling reflects the current-new data-flow off the archived-old Experience-Senses and delivers Mind-Self attraction-gradient assessments to both response patterning systems (via **Test-It**s) and the **Movie-of-Your-Life** presentation center.

Even if there is no sight, as in a dark room or over the phone, one's Devise-Mulling formulates an impression based on available sensory-acceptance.

Sensory-assessment is so powerful that even while watching a movie one evaluates the actors 'character' by assimilating micro-motions and facial expressions.

Believable actors have the ability to 'get deeply into character', which means they believe they are the part and therefore their granular expressions are contiguous with the scene being created.

Conversely, bad acting causes us to use our imagination, which really means filling in the missing pieces from one's own insufficient data-archives. Resultantly, we feel dissatisfied with the production, as our 'personality' is discordant with the stories characters.

The streaming detail, as is the case for all cognitive data-flow is ultimately handled in the Movie-of-Your-Life arena where it is blended and displayed in the cognitive appropriate second-by-second timeframe: not in the millisecond-by-millisecond timeframe.

Actions performed, not obscure intentions, define a person. Interestingly, when micro-actions (Body motions) are folded into the mix of larger physical-actions (speaking, etc.), they explain why one finds some folks appealing, and others not so much.

As the first two books proved, genetics provides the neural predisposition baseplate. In other words, the DNA template actualizes each type of data-archive neuron and the parameters within which each operates.

Notably, the acceptable frequency or Matched-Base-Frequency characteristic is most relevant for these discussions.

Additionally though, we are born with neither populated Matched-Base-Frequencies nor Base-one through Base-five data-archives. Instead, compatible data-archives must be populated by variously intense action-potentials originating as sensory-acceptance.

Thus, attraction-revulsion gradient can range from visceral (Body-Self) when one's experiences are scarce, to cognitive (Mind-Self) when one has great familiarity.

The visceral response is real. It is genetically designed to rapidly assess events and objects in one's Bombardment-Sphere (environment), which may pose a threat.

The Cognitive evaluation, comparing current-new to archived-old is the result of either Cognitive-Self assessing a Cognitive-Alert from Body-Self and/or from Cognitive-Sensors (visual) providing additional sensory fodder.

When assessment corroborates or even intensifies the imperative-alert (Cognitive-Alert data-package), which indicates threat, one's Cognitive-Habits react with avoidance responses that tend to evaluate toward the revulsion side of the gradient, which in turn produces Test-Its formatted for flight and/or fight.

However, with either a request-alert or when Cognitive-Complex downplays the current-new data-package (due to visual sensor input) one tends to evaluate toward the attraction side of the gradient, which in turn produces Test-Its formatted to be inquisitive.

On the high side of the range of possible outcomes or responses is attraction, likes etc.: on the low side, repulsion and dislikes.

Remember, Cognitive-Self is much slower, so by the time it reacts Body-Self has inspired potentially thousands of miniscule Soma-Actions that have already initialized the journey to a less threatening position within one's Bombardment-Sphere.

Thus, both Habit-Duo members operate in concert. To keep us safe genetic predisposition provides the facilities that enable acquisition (data-archived action-potentials), retention and Recognition-Analysis.

When one person is attracted to another they normally state something like: 'there is just something in the way she/he moves, speaks, looks, talks, etc. that attracts me. Attraction is also not just a single point of reference but presents as a gradient from mild to extreme, which I call the **attraction-gradient**. Resultantly, although you might be extremely attracted to someone, they might be blasé toward you.

So how does attraction work? What are its determiners?

As underlined in the first two books, there are two pervasive determiners of "everything we are and everything we can become": genetics, which provides the capacity; and data-archives, which storehouse potentially retrievable fodder 'substance'.

In that Homo Sapien genetics has less than one-half of one percent variance between people and attraction variance can be huge, genetics can be justifiably ruled out as the sole cause. So, what is the additional attraction driver then besides appearance?

Only one other choice exists: data-archive population.

In other words, the way one's data-archives have been populated due to one's lifelong interaction with their Bombardment-Sphere is the additional determiner. Let's delve to see how data-archive population could be responsible for attraction outcomes.

Firstly, when you newly meet someone, all sensory-acceptance is current-new: therefore, it has no exact data-archive counterpart. We also know that Body-Self always compares current-new to archived-old to evaluate dichotomously whether events being sensory-accepted from one's Bombardment-Sphere are recognized or **UN**-recognized.

Additionally, when **UN**-recognized, Body-Self always sends a Cognitive-Alert to Mind-Self for assistance with the 'problematic' issue. In this case, let's assume the Cognitive-Alert is a **request-alert** and therefore not survival threatening.

Resultantly, Mind-Self gets busy doing its thing, which involves creating Puzzle-sets, bringing its sensors (vision) on-line to gather additional information and accessing its corresponding data-archives for **significantly-similar**: Herein is a primary Key for attraction.

To find out why, we need to probe into what sensory-events actually populated frequency applicable **significantly-similar** data-archives.
Herein enters our most powerful driver: **Habit-Power**. Both pro-habits and chaos-habits have been populated by sensory-acceptance from birth to now.

Stands to reason that the habits with the greatest **GO-TO** strength (highest action-potential energy) are also those that continue to be flooded with action-potentials.

Also though, duration is a huge factor. The longer one is exposed to a repetitive set of circumstances the 'larger' or more intense are the data-archives associated with the repetitive sensory-events.

Susceptibility is also a factor. When was one most easily influenced?

That of course would be when related data-archives were minimal or contained negligible action-potential. The susceptibility-gradient timeframe of course is about 100% at birth and diminishes as we approach adulthood.

> Keep in mind though any time in life when one does not have sufficient experience (i.e., sufficiently populated data-archives for broad-scope evaluation), susceptibility is fairly much at maximum. This is why one can be convinced about the credibility of something that is bogus from self-interested salespeople to investment scams.

Putting the pieces together then, domestication has provided the foundations for the vast majority of one's original GO-TO data-archives. Thus, they become the comfort-zone cognitively-habitual 'norms'.

> What you liked or hated as a child are part of your data-archives. If you felt loved, then love is the GO-TO; if abused, avoidance is the GO-TO: If your parents were overweight; you probably struggle with weight issues, etc.

Whatever existed in your young environment thus molded your Mind-Self data-archives. Thus, of Mind-Self's five data-archive Tiers, Experience-Senses (Tier-5) are not only the least malleable but also, as we have learned, storehouse Cognitive-Habits, which are the primary initial and rapid cognitive-responders to current-new.

In other words, Cognitive-Habits form our assumptive-thinking survival strategy or 'first-blush' nature. As this is their mandate, Cognitive-Habits immediately drive 'tinted' Test-Its to interface with Body-Self Soma-Actions.

Resultantly, as the Test-Its are compromised by Cognitive-Habit biases, so too will the feedback that is purposed to get more information for ratification or reversal assessment be swayed.

Thus, when you meet someone and current-new is interlaced with domesticated archived-old, corresponding significantly-similar Experience-Senses are activated.

> When most or all activated Experience-Senses are pleasant, attraction is great; when few activate, attraction is minimal.

Thus, someone's physical features ('looks') and their micro-motions, which form current-new are what spirit data-archive retrieval, which thus determines Cognitive-Habit assumptive attraction-gradient positioning: along the scale from initial attraction, to disregard, to repulsion.

When contact results in detraction though, the likelihood of your investing additional time, which could confirm or refute initial Experience-Sense assumptions, is unlikely.

> In other words, Experience-Senses are so pervasively in control, you will seldom give someone a second chance to make a first impression.

Disregard occurs also because once sensory-acceptance becomes recognized and lower-intensity Soma-habits kick in and thus Cognitive-Alerts are never issued. Therefore, because Cognitive-Pathway 3 does not re-engage, one looks away.

Consequently, one ignores the source, which in this case is the person assessed as ho-hum.

Even if you did force yourself to reassess, it would be a long road of data-archive populating to create new more lenient Tier-5 **GO-TO** Experience-Senses, as these Cognitive-Habits always assume they are correct.

Questionable 'Chooser'

This takes us to the consequences of having chaos-habit Experience-Senses or Cognitive-Habits mixed into the evaluation pool by Devise-Mulling's independent interpreter.

Recall, 'independent' in this context means when Devise-Mulling is ferreting or mulling without too much reliance (or any) on current-new information. This can be transparent as in dreams or active as in consciously choosing to engage in activities.

Everyone has said something like; I should never have gotten involved because I had a gut feeling this person (or activity) was just wrong.

When one mistrusts their feelings (see intuition discussions), which we know from Book-one are the pivotal underpinning of all action-potentials and thus data-archives as well, choices will be questionable, especially when the self-doubt chaos-habit is strong.

> In the absence of good information: all information seems good.

The solution then is to gather as much information and reputable opinions as possible. This should offset the tendency, which allows chaos-habit soaked Devise-Mulling **Test-It**s to negatively impact actions.

> In other words, think twice, act once: Instead of acting once and then regretting multiple decisions.

One is not stupid by either taking time to evaluate and/or scoping-out expert sources. The acting rashly chaos-habit alternate though (i.e., inadequate experience gathering) will certainly result in damaging not only your Public-Self image but also your Private-Self competency beliefs.

If you are in doubt about the values each should either bring to the table or agree to create together, I have included the following Relationship-Guide. It has helped many, many couples define important relationship building blocks that enhance their joint and individual living-experiences.

Relationship Guideline (Desiderata)

Create a reciprocally inclusive pro-habit relationship:

Where interaction is involved, considerate, kind, compassionate and caring
Where the needs and feelings of the other are as significant as your own
Where agreements, not decrees are the basis of interaction
Where there is full disclosure without secrets
Where there are no hidden agendas
Where compliments flow freely
Where trust is unbreakable

Where decisions are made together over whatever time is necessary
to ensure inclusion.

Where there is an overwhelming desire to give and receive
love and belonging.

Where commitment to the other is unshakable
Where nurturing, not sabotage is the rule
Where sensitivity, not neglect pervades

Where partners can show mutual appreciation of the gifts each
is bestowing upon the other.

Lobster-Fork Relationship Model

Although the Relationship-Decagon is ever present and each person certainly needs to integrate and agree on selected aspects of the Relationship-Guide presented above, a simpler alternate is additionally available. Pertinent for couples or multiple members within two negotiating groups, I call this perspective the Lobster-Fork Model.

Couples

By definition, couples are two people who have come together with sufficient passion and interest in one another's lifestyle to form a group of two.

In the Lobster-Fork Model then, where the lobster-forks two tines flow together to form a handle or base of somewhat 'equal' length, the tines represent the individual, whereas the base represents the group (of two). In other words, two tines symbolize two people: the integrated base their natural or agreed overlap.

Overlap is defined as those aspects that have been mutually decided (without reservation) as acceptable by both individuals: even though an individual, if still single might have exercised a different conclusion.

> Overlaps are many in a cooperative relationship: They span from furniture choices to décor, to cleanliness, to friends, to body type, to fitness level, etc.

When we meet someone, keeping in mind 'Attraction' discussions above, we are comforted by their similarities but excited about their differences. Therefore, at the start of an intimate relationship one explores and more importantly celebrates and participates in each other's differences (maybe hiking, sailing, movie types, foods, etc.) and revel in similarities that sustain comfort.

Unfortunately, as a couple-relationship becomes more familiar, chaos-habits (such as control, disregard and impatience) can come to roost between the tines. When these and other chaos-habits manifest they may not only obliterate a clear view of the others intentions and desires but also grow so large that the pressure cracks and tears the handle apart.

So, what can be done to avoid such a break?

Firstly, be aware that individual chaos-habits exist. Secondly, just because you both form a group, where each is genuinely attempting to create mutual loving and caring pro-habits, does not mean that individual chaos-habits will just go away.

What needs to be accomplished is to grow the action-potential of newly forming group pro-habits (such as loving, respect, courtesy, benefit of the doubt, kindness, no blame, and the like from the Relationship Guide) so they mostly become the **GO-TO**'s instead.
Now aware of the Relationship Decagon and Relationship Guide, passionate diligence and practice are of course Key to successfully aspiring new individual and group pro-habits to **GO-TO** status.

> Why passion (excitement of mutually becoming enlightened), practice and diligence: Because they are pivotal to quickly scooping adequate action-potential to sufficiently populate respective data-archives, so you can both get what you **TRULY** want?

Do not try to fake it: avoidance of passionate and committed deployment will not work because your sensory-scoop will simply be too small to provide sufficient fodder to create **GO-TO** pro-habits powerful enough to usurp well-established chaos-habits.

The resistance chaos-habit will try to keep you in place for sure. It will summon all sorts of comrades such as denial, chagrin and dismissal. Do not let those old chaos-habits outdo and undo you though.

> Instead, stay the course and I guarantee … that which seemed hard at first will become easy: **this is after all the Habit gift**!

Thirdly, celebrate, inspire and be respectful of your partners differences. Not only will this be appreciated by your partner but also both of your self-esteem pro-habits will be foddered and therefore begin to disengage its self-doubt chaos-habit nemesis. In other words, you will both feel better about yourselves as well as the other.

Besides, the excitement of wholeheartedly engaging with your partner in their passions will serve to broaden your perspectives by foddering as yet untapped new data-archives.

Keep in mind … broader perspectives equals better choosing; and better choosing dramatically spirits you both on the path to get what you **TRULY** want!

Gifts into Requirements

This section is not meant to insult anyone. Instead, the intention is to spirit awareness that more-useful pro-habit choices are possible for both partners.

By way of example, I repeatedly witness what I consider a major chaos-habit relationship killer: turning gifts into requirements.

In a relationship, both partners are at times guilty of disregarding the value of the gifts being provided by the other: i.e., everyday niceties freely given out of caring and respect for the benefit of the other.

Everyone likes to be recognized for kindnesses. This predilection stands to reason because, as we have learned from the first two books all of one's neuro-physiological processes provision a 'recognized / UN-recognized' essential evaluative component. Therefore, so too do one's Experience-Senses or Cognitive-Habits.

One major key to a fulfilling relationship is to ensure that you do not become numb or disconnected as to gift value. When someone does something nice for you reciprocate, especially when it's not expected: Both will feel way better than if gifts are received as required.

'Requirement' and its chaos-habit siblings, expectation and entitlement are huge problems in a relationship because they preclude recognition for beneficial gifted actions freely given for the partners benefit. Make no mistake, when one ignores another's kind actions or regards those gifted actions as no big deal, it is disrespectful, insulting and neglectful.

Remember … no matter how hard you neglect a relationship:
It is not going to get better!

Gift actions, to be acknowledged, should not be evaluated as large, small or even enormously useful: genuinely valued with a sincere thank-you and future reciprocation.

From my perspective, I will detail one gift-dismissing activity, turning a gift into a requirement, which I observe frequently.

First off, I do not mean to pick on women. I get there are many females out there who do not feel appreciated: To this, I can only say, "smarten-up males and read on".

Without question, women like having certain niceties genuinely performed by their partner: like paying for meals, letting them go first through doors, opening car doors, telling them they are attractive, etc. There is nothing wrong with liking these kindnesses. Most males love **DO**ing things for their women.

I tend to eat out quite a bit both with friends and while travelling to speak. Over decades, with the specific purpose of observing when and if a particular gift-recognition is offered, I have observed hundreds of couples across a broad cultural spectrum. Understanding gift-recognition behaviour is additionally important to me, as gift-recognition is a central topic I highlight in couples and family counselling.

Whether standing in line at a fast food or sitting in a posh establishment, my observations support that the male pays more than 85% of the time: No problem with that. Certainly, this activity has all the characteristics of a gift: time, thoughtfulness, effort, etc.

Here is the difficulty. When the relationship looks 'established', I seldom observe a thank you from the partner to acknowledge the males considerate action.

I am convinced the perceptions that drive gift dismissive attitudes are due to domestication. Although domestication probably began in the home, it is continually reinforced by female role models from movies and sitcoms to the internet and magazines.

> As domestication is the culprit, the good news is that once identified each person can create new respectful pro-habits, which acknowledge rather than disregard the gifts of the other.

Fellows: When you get home and your mate has prepared a meal or done anything, that directly or indirectly benefit to you, provide huge and sincere thanks!

The appreciation and recognition you genuinely give will enhance both of your individual and partnership living-experiences by spiriting deeper insight into each other's Private-Selves.

Gift-to-Requirement Scenario

I will clarify by way of an anecdote.

Syllivan and her husband Ean are very happy together. Their mutual respect and admiration is obvious to all they know. Each intently and genuinely enjoys listening to the other when talking: even when very familiar with the story. They are kind, helpful, participate when the other requests and are obviously interested in benefiting the other whenever possible.

Ean has a favorite gift he has enjoyed giving for a couple of years since their marriage: he brings flowers every Friday evening that Syllivan excitedly appreciates. Ean feels good just by gifting the flowers and deeply appreciates his partners excited gratitude.

Syllivan on the other hand feels loved and appreciated due to not only the energy and thought Ean obviously puts into 'flower-giving' but also because she feels warmly recognized for all she does.

Ean's perception however of his spontaneous gift giving to express his love and appreciation for Syllivan was about to be shattered.

His route home last evening, Friday, was cordoned off for a square mile or so due to a water-main break. The detour was way out of his way through farmland back roads.

It took an additional hour through nightmarish stop-and-start crawling traffic, which did afford Ean time to text Syllivan about the problem.

an arrived home frustrated but happy. It was finally the weekend that Syllivan and he had been looking forward to for some time: They were going boating together for the first time.

He came in, gave Syllivan his normal huge smile and hug, chatted a little about the travel home conditions and asked about Syllivans day.

She remained uncharacteristically quiet and illusive for about 30 seconds and dropped the bombshell: "Where are my flowers – didn't you get me flowers she complained"?

In that moment, Ean felt his world collapse. He had thought the flowers were a wonderful gift freely given and freely received. Now however, he felt with stomach sickening upset that the flowers were not being received as a spontaneous gift to show his love and appreciation at all but was a requirement to prove his love.

Point is … do not change a beautiful gift into a requirement: it will always make the other person feel used, sad and unappreciated.

Even though a simplified story, similar scenarios play out far too often by both men and women. Notably, the chaos-habit of entitlement instead of the pro-habit of appreciation is a relationship trust killer.

In other words, entitlement calls into question whether everything one happily does for another is actually a requirement not a gift. This chaos-habit is emotionally impacting because one Experience-Senses dissonance: the difference between the way you thought something was and the way you get jolted into understanding it actually is.

> The requirement chaos-habit will always have disrupting consequences, whereas the gift-giving pro-habit will provide great joy.

I suggest probing your arsenal of responses and then working on disenfranchising the entitlement chaos-habit by enhancing your appreciation pro-habit. I guarantee that both your relationship with yourself and with others will result in huge benefit to your living-experience.

> Appreciation fodders happiness and fulfillment:
> Requirement fodders sadness and discontent.
>
> Notably, tolerating is NOT appreciation but condescension.

Additionally, most who feel unfulfilled and unappreciated will seek resolution elsewhere.

Sender and Receiver

Firstly, as discussed earlier, recall that speaking is just noise. One only has to listen to people speaking an unfamiliar foreign language to verify that.

Secondly, one has auditory sensory-arrays attuned to first receiving the inbound mechanical energy of noise and then converting it into electrical energy or action-potential.

Soon after birth, one begins the lifelong practice of trying to correctly interpret noises.

As we are a habitual-species, practice means that one creates data-archives for a genetically determined mandate, which is to evaluate the current-new, in this case noise, as either recognized or **UN**-recognized for the purposes of either remaining safe or responding oneself to safety (hopefully rapidly and somewhat appropriately).

> For instance, unlikely a newborn would react to someone screaming. However, it does not take long, if screaming is perpetuated, for the maturing infant to build appropriate data-archives that will habitually kick-in and thus react with upset upon a new occurrence.

Thirdly, sensory-array conversion is only the first of many morphing's. One's neural array Cognitive-Pathways are busy places. They are continually utilizing the ever 'flowing' current-new to locate significantly-similar archived-old matches, which are used as comparatives.

Fourthly, **significantly-similar** as discussed does not mean **SAME**: thus significantly-similar retrieval can vary substantially – even be erroneous - based on such circumstances as topic, familiarity, current Bombardment-Sphere conditions, context, health, self-doubt and so on.

> I recently went through a golden arches drive through where I ordered a 'cone'. However, when I reached the dispensing window, I was handed a 'coke'. After explaining that the item was incorrect, the young fellow apologized by saying: "Sorry…no-one has ever ordered a cone from me before… but hundreds of cokes".

Thus, one does not 'hear the actual noise'. Instead, one 'hears-the-spin' created by many cerebral processors, which first morph current-new via significantly-similar retrieval and then filter findings through Experience-Sense or Cognitive-Habit prisms that ultimately determine perception.

> This is also why when you say a sentence to someone and ask each member of a line of ten or so to pass it along, it is dramatically morphed.

In a conversation between two people, with the above points in mind, two roles flip-flop: the Sender or the one speaking and the Receiver or the one hearing.

Notice I did not say listening but hearing. This is an important distinction because the act of hearing is a sensory-array capability whereas listening is a developed skill or pro-habit set.

> First, seek to understand: then be understood.

As with all sensory information that inspires Cognitive-Alerts, the current-new / archived-old assembly is subject to Cognitive-Habit filtering.

In other words, Cognitive-Habit prisms bias perception by eliminating **UN**-recognized: i.e., those frequencies that do not match its Tier-5 data-archive constructs. Thus, its outbound Test-It configurations then actually fabricate reality.

> Resultantly, one often hears something like: "I don't think you heard me quite right" or "let me restate that".

The result is Cognitive-Habits determine what is 'heard' by devising its own outbounds or Test-Its. Thus arise the assumptive-thinking chaos-habit where one allows their Cognitive-Habits to form **micro-conclusions** as a message is being delivered.

This process is definitely not useful for either communicator as it invariably ends in the Receiver interrupting and the Sender being frustrated with incomplete delivery: its disrespectful and should be replaced with the Pro-habit of listening.

Let's redefine the skill of Pro-habit listening then to include among other aspects: respectful attention by the Receiver, patience to allow the sender full topic presentation, absence of **micro-assessments** and micro-conclusions and the inclusion of pertinent questions toward comprehensive understanding.

When being understood is the goal, the Sender also has responsibility. Specifically, to communicate and re-communicate, i.e., rephrase projected noises, as long as the Receiver is willing to accept. Especially with committed couples, it is imperative that the impatience chaos-habit be kept dormant.

We are a receiving species: more specifically sensory-arrays must be sufficiently activated before we notice anything. Furthermore, depending on Experience-Sense biases as to current-new acceptability or frequency fit of both the current-new to archived-old assessment and current-new intensity the content is morphed and thus perceived according to one's Cognitive-Habits.

> Quickly assuming to know the other's meaning is oftentimes wrong: at least at the granular level where most of the exciting-new exists.

Just as with music and art do not assume that all the textures you are 'hearing' i.e., processing current-new to archived-old are the same between people because as we have learned, the Cognitive-Self archived-old reflective surface can be substantially different one person to the next due to wide varying experiences.

However, other dynamics are at play that each should try to accommodate as well: such as, conversation timing, delivery speed, intonation, urgency, topic and speech complexity, subject familiarity, repetition, patience, monologue timeframes, duration of interactions and so on.

 The creation of conversational pro-habits are critical to master because in their void is only misunderstanding and frustration.

Speakers: tailor communications for the receiver. When your perspective is unfamiliar to your partner, respectfully allow them to come up to speed by patiently providing small enough snippets in an environment of fun discussion to appreciate your point-of-view.

Do not require them to agree … that is unreasonable. However, reasonable is to seek their understanding. Sustain a love and belonging posture. Allow passion and spirited conversation: do not mistake this for threatening … retrain your flight chaos-habits.

Don't 'you-too': it's sets up defensiveness and controversy rather than mutual solutioning.

Don't try and win because then your partner and you both lose. There is little that is right or wrong or good or bad: Just useful or not-so-useful. So strive for useful as much as possible.

Always be inclusive rather than exclusive.

We have been deceived that anger is a valid emotion: it is not. There is absolutely no resolution possible in anger.

Instead, develop the Pro-habit of wedging an ever widening **time-space** between an event that you deem noxious, and your chosen action to resolve it. That way you get to choose from constructive arrays of positive and supportive options rather than be dictated to by responding with destructive domesticated chaos-habits.

Do not nurture and drag your past into your Present:
So doing will absolutely mess up your Present and your Future.

The past does not physically exist anymore than the future.

The only reason past events seems real to you is that your Chatterbox self-doubt chaos-habits, which have been programmed by domestication to diminish you, have been given permission **by you** to regurgitate and dump old history (archived-old) into your current-event stream.

This **aberrant recall** chaos-habit is what is keeping you from becoming all you can be by interjecting compulsive, destructive and addictive interlopers into Test-It outbounds as if they are current-new.

> Pinch those hoses and do not tolerate or accept the nonsense they are trying to feed you: that you are not good enough. You are!

Health: Mental and Physical

Mental

One useful definition of good mental health is an unshakable feeling of well-being. Such feelings derive from established Private-Self // Public-Self pro-habits, which support that you are competent capable of handling whatever random Bombardment-Sphere events are fired your way.

In other words, regardless of turmoil, which arrives on everyone's doorstep, the experiences will not defeat but strengthen your resolve that you are worthy and capable, either singularly or by requesting assistance.

What will surely get in the way of best-scenario handling of difficult events is actually not one's capability but instead domesticated chaos-habits, such as self-doubt, whose Chatterbox companion convinces that you are neither sufficiently worthy or competent nor good enough.

Upon being assaulted by some disruptive event, when first feelings are defeat and fear and/or you resort to addictions like smoking, drugs anger and/or other not-so-useful behaviours, you can be sure your domesticated chaos-habits are in charge.

Do not beat yourself up for not-so-useful behaviours, as that would be succumbing to the self-doubt chaos-habit. Instead, take the opportunity to move toward the event instead of away from it. This will begin to not only disenfranchise self-doubt but also initiate the capability pro-habit.

Remember, only by sensory-data gathering does one populate data-archives or gain experience. Indubitably then, by approaching a 'fearful event' you will engage both Cognition-Complex and Devise-Mulling and thus gain enormous experience: regardless of whether you wanted it or not.

The alternate is some form of running away (either physically and/or to the false comfort of addictions), which of course engage Chatterbox whose self-recrimination wheelhouse will continue to create you and rule your days.

Although it sounds trite, attempt to use all events that come your way to build self-esteem pro-habit sets and disengage damaging chaos-habits, such as the self-doubt dictator. Absolutely ask others to help. Trust me; they will be more than happy to assist.

Additionally, every time your Chatterbox pipes up, tell it in a **loud firm voice** to shut-up and go away. By doing this you will begin disengaging this chaos-habit and begin creating a new 'I am in control, not you' pro-habit.

Absolutely, do not take anything your Chatterbox has to say as either true or useful.

Remember Chatterbox is just a Cognitive-Habit: and we now understand we can create our own more useful **GO-TO** pro-habits, while at the same time diminishing the effectiveness of our chaos-habits.

Both outcomes can be accomplished by **DO**ing. Specifically, you can achieve resolution by not only adjusting our Bombardment-Sphere position to gather more useful Deluge but also purposefully or consciously engaging Devise-Mulling to create Puzzles and **Test-IT**s that empower rather than marginalise your living-experiences.

> Literally, and in every way - the choice to create pro-habits to get you what you **TRULY** want and disengage **GO-TO** chaos-habits that result in an unfulfilled you - is 100% up to you.

Physical

Therefore, to enhance mental and physical health do some, all or more of the following. Join groups where you have fun; go dancing and dance lots; join your community centre and take in some of their Zumba-type classes; stand more – sit less; park the car far away from entrances and walk briskly.

Additionally, play SUDOKU as it keeps Devise-Mulling Puzzle creation strong, which is the main reason I wrote it (alright this is a plug for my **Become a SUDOKU Master** books, but valid none-the-less); the list is almost endless.

Simultaneous to above actions, you will probably need to create a new fitness pro-habit set. Getting and staying healthy is mandatory: so eat sensibly, get exercise and drink lots of water.

Know that the lethargy chaos-habit set along with Chatterbox are resilient. They will try to rationalize you out of doing anything new. However, by being diligent for 5 to 15 days, these **GO-TO** chaos-habits will begin their decline into obscurity.
Why eat sensibly?

No sense upping your metabolism by exercising in order to burn calories over the next 24 hours, if you cancel out the fitness-effect by going for either a big meal (or elaborate barista drink) afterwards or starve your body of its number one ingredient, water. Remember, water is responsible for about 75% of your body weight, so it is an obvious critical component.

Weight Management

> Losing weight is a matter of ensuring calories in (those being consumed or eaten) is less than calories out (those metabolically burned).

When overweight, it is typically caused by what I abbreviate as **ETM / ETL**: Eating-Too-Much and Exercising-Too-Little.

Getting in shape is attainable by simply 'breaking-a-sweat' (just a little is fine) three or four time a week for about 20 minutes: **However, it does not have to be consecutive minutes**.

The twenty-minutes can be made up of 5 minutes here and 5 minutes there throughout the day. How simple is that!

For instance, **briskly** walk up and down steps instead of using elevators or escalators and/or energetically walk from place to place in your house instead of just sauntering.

> As a matter of principle, right now decide that sauntering (movement without breaking a little sweat or breathing a little harder) is out and energetic movement is in.

One domesticated chaos-habit set, let's call it the body-look chaos-habit is resiliently dominant. It is a direct consequence of how your parents physically looked when you were young and has thus been reinforced for decades.

Consider when you were at your most impressionable age range, eight to eighteen, your parents were somewhere in the range of thirty to fifty years old: give or take.

Being dependent on parents for most everything throughout life one typically cares for and love their parents. Because you love your parents the way they look is accepted without question. The rub is that your acceptance is creating a physical-acceptability chaos-habit set.

So, when parents are overweight and/or lethargic, these Experience-Senses or Cognitive-Habits will become instilled, as they are normal to you. Interestingly, when you reach age 40ish, you will begin to actually behave and look-like you're your parents.

In other words, these 'normal-to-you' traits will manifest because cognitive-habit filtering will not perceive these chaos-habits as unacceptable.

Thus, overweight parents typically have overweight children: Not just because of poor diet and lack of exercise but more because the parents fitness level 'seems' normal or is Experience-Sensed as acceptable. In other words, as overweight and lethargic seems normal, few flags go up alerting there is a better way.

Ones gradients-of-normality across an extensive variety of subjects are of course Cognitive-Habits, which as we know will vehemently enforce (as do all Habits) their 'middle-of-the-flume' mandates to both steadfastly exert their fixed agendas and remain the **GO-TO**'s.

Poor diet and lack of exercise are chaos-habits. They continually enforce their status-quo agendas (this is their inherent design) by downgrading current-new intensity and restricting archived-old retrieval.

In other words, any attempts to change to good diet and get exercise will be countered with **habit-resistance**.

Habit-resistance takes the form of anxiety, justification, temptation, denial and many other frequency-associated chaos-habits that are tenaciously conjured to keep you functioning within habit-driven not choice-driven parameters.

Such **Habit-Force** is great when it comes to enforcing pro-habits that are automatically getting you what you truly want (like a degree or gold medal) but disastrous when damaging chaos-habits (like self-doubt, anger and addictions) are causing havoc to your living-experiences.

Turn-the-Tables

Fortunately, three **How-We-Work** absolutes or Keys are available to turn-the-table from chaos-habits creating you to your creating pro-habits that will dramatically enhance living-experiences. These principles, which use the tenacious nature of Cognitive chaos-habits, enable one to create simultaneously pro-habits that will get you what you TRULY want and disarm chaos-habits that are wreaking havoc.

First, **triggered-behaviour** (Cognitive-Habits) is a direct consequence of sensory-accepted events or current-new that occurred within your Bombardment-Sphere.

Second, in order to rapid respond all events will be evaluated as either recognized or **UN**-recognized by cerebral processors.

Thirdly, we know Experience-Senses (Cognitive-Habits) are the Mind-Self's rapid cognitive responders, which utilize Tier-five 'Normals' to significantly influence one's actual outbound behaviours.

Although we can directly do little about Recognition-Analysis or Experience-Senses being mixed into outbound rapid-response Test-Its, we have some control at the Bombardment-Sphere source.

In other words, you have the choice-capability via Devise-Mulling to adjust Bombardment-Sphere conditions: and thus directly alter sensory-acceptance.

> Excitingly, this strategy provides not only the means to avoid your chaos-habit 'recognized' triggers but also the potential to create pro-habits.

For instance, if you have a junk food gourmand chaos-habit (i.e., like to eat way too much) that manifests when you sit in your normal spot to watch T.V. continually change the triggering environment until the temptation chaos-habit is no longer the **GO-TO**.

Following are a few suggestions to initialize the process of not only disarming chaos-habit triggers, which manifest due to your Bombardment-Sphere presenting **recognized and lower-intensity** events but also creating new pro-habits.

Recall that by positional modification within your Bombardment-Sphere, you are actually changing sensory-accepted frequencies. Thus, you are literally freeing yourself from recognized and lower-intensity events, which drive Soma-habits, and instead promoting **UN-recognized and/or higher-intensity** that spirits Cognitive-Alerts, which instigate Mind-Self to Figure-It-Out by Puzzle creation and Solutioning.

That's why adjustments 'feel' different. You are not responding Habitually but instead Cognitively Solutioning and creating new Cognitive (Mind-Self) data-archives, Experience-Senses, Template-Patterns and Cognitive-Responses.

If you really want to Experience-Sense how Bombardment-Sphere adjustments can dramatically change the way you 'feel', flip your position on the couch: head where your feet would normally be.

Trust me, if you pay attention, you can actually 'feel' or Experience-Sense Puzzle creation, feedback-loops as you attempt the reversal, new perceptions, etc.: so totally exciting you will remember every detail and have a great story to tell.

Here are a few other Bombardment-Sphere adjustments you can try: rearrange the room; sit in different spots; manipulate spongy balls; knit; stand instead of sit; limit watching T.V. to one hour on - one hour off; alternate giving your partner neck and shoulder massages (keeps your hands busy); etc.

Additional to the above, in order to interrupt those eating-frenzy chaos-habits: sip room temperature water (cold water increases metabolism and triggers chemoreceptors responsible for hunger); eat an apple or banana instead of chips; make a protein shake with fruit juice; make your stepper or treadmill part of your T.V. watching process; etc.

While creating beneficial pro-habits do not forget to be creative and get excited: remember, creative flourishes **UN**-recognized events, which do not trigger chaos-habits; while excited builds the new pro-habit data-archive way, way more quickly, which results in a pro-habit becoming the **GO-TO** faster.

Such is Habit-Power!

You can definitely utilize **Habit-Power** every minute of every day to *WayBetter* Your L.I.F.E^2.!

Wealth: Joyfulness and Material

Attainment of Wealth – both types - is symmetrically dependent on the persistence-gradient of your self-doubt chaos-habit. This is why presentation of Wealth is last.

Whether exerting weak or strong influence, the consequences of the self-doubt chaos-habit set are damaging. Its **GO-TO** control effectiveness simply begets different levels of debilitation.

> In other words, when you strongly self-doubt your worthiness - meaning the self-doubt chaos-habit set is mostly the **GO-TO** driver - then belief that you do not deserve joy or 'stuff' will be congruently pronounced.

As wealth of either type must be believed as possible by you, for you, any erosion of conviction will correspondingly water-down your **DO**ing. Reduced **DO**ing is a problem because sensory-acceptance due to reduced interactions with the **Out-There** simply does not provide sufficient fodder for **Figuring-It-Out** and finding **The-Ways**.

Therefore, passions that are imperative to get you what you **TRULY** want cannot manifest. Consequently, both data-acquisition and recall are crippled, which makes difficult not only learning and creating pro-habits but also recall. When recall is inhibited so are the quantity and intensity of outbound Test-Its, which are responsible for feedback, symmetrically limited.

Thus, because the **Out-There** resultantly seems unfriendly in these conditions, coping will replace joy and excitement, which additionally severely limits interactions.

When feeling unworthy, Cognitive-habits actually shun even the **UN**-recognized and/or higher-intensity current-new frequencies that are outside chaos-habit gradients-of-acceptability (i.e., outside a chaos-habits data-archive harmonic frequency range). In other words, chaos-habits retreat you into your comfort zone where they 'rule-the-day' by ensuring nothing new or exciting is perceived and new **DO**ing is minimized.

> Recognizable as resistive behaviour (chaos-habit) think of a time recently – maybe someone trying to show you a new cellphone feature – where as soon as they suggested the possibility not only did your anxiety skyrocket but also you fabricated some excuse to avoid the learning situation (too busy right now is a favorite).

As the situation did not 'fit' your currently dominant Cognitive chaos-habit set frequencies, the new information was thus denied and ignored: result - minimal action and excitement.

Causing additional degradation to your living-experiences are intertwined chaos-habit sets such as lethargy, hiding, and fear. They will, due to the extensive processing necessary to reject 'unacceptable' current-new, suck-up any remaining metabolic energy.

The Hiding chaos-habit compounds your negative sense of self-worth by presenting highly edited and limited information to the Movie-of-Your-L.I.F.E. processing arenas, which thereby deceives that everything is either all right and will get better or the universe will provide.

The preferred alternate would be to create and or strengthen your acceptance pro-habit (and its companion's, involvement, interest and excitement). Trust me; they are a lot more fun!

Joyfulness

Let me strongly purport that the universe has already delivered big time!

Specifically, for whatever unknown combination of universe laws, **Universe-H** has provided miracles in the form of two of the greatest gifts possible: **choice**, enabling improvement to one's living-conditions and **mobility**, which sanctions almost unlimited capabilities to **DO**.

> **Key** then is to utilize choice and mobility fervently to *WayBetter* Your L.I.F.E^2.!

So, now we understand that **DO**ing is key to joyfulness and that **DO**ing is almost boundless due to physical mobility and choice (capability to formulate unlimited Devise-Mulling Puzzles to Solution – i.e., Figure-It-Out and find The-Ways), what are some pro-habits we can cultivate that will *WayBetter* Your L.I.F.E^2.?

Keeping previous discussions in mind, a short list follows, which is designed to inspire your Devise-Mulling arsenal: Talk-happy; immerse yourself in whatever you choose to DO; compliment rather than criticise; appreciate others; exercise and stay in shape; eat to live – don't eat to eat; join groups; find those who cherish you … avoid those who don't; be of service to others without being a servant; imagine and dream all sorts of fantastic things; dance; acquire the humor perspective; **DO** community service; play sports (even if its shuffleboard); 100% engage with your partner; share ideas; expand your perspectives by trying uncomfortable things; work to strengthen pro-habits that get you what you TRULY want; avoid feeding debilitating chaos-habits. Feel free to add more.

Material

Much has been written about getting 'stuff'. However, in regard to our goal of creating pro-habits that easily get you what you **TRULY** want and disengaging chaos-habits that disrupt that quest, following are a few simple perspectives and easy to deploy suggestions to get you on the pro-habit, material wealth creating highway.

Keep in mind **TRULY** is not equal to 'kina-sorta'. **TRULY** means absolutely passionate and committed, so that when unexpected cracks (small or big) in your dream fulfillment highway occur, you will not stop but instead find a way around it, over it or throw a plank, a tree-trunk or a jury-bridge across it.

In other words, **TRULY** means whatever it takes you are dedicated to getting across: i.e., Figuring-It-Out and finding The-Ways.

TRULY is the Key to all success.

Proceeding without **TRULY** is like putting ice in your beverage on a hot day: it just melts and waters down your beverage until it becomes yuck.

Do not expect to get 100% out of an energy system, if you only put 80% in: that is neither possible nor reasonable.

No question: Dream fulfillment takes ALL of your passion – start to finish.

Success happens through persistence: greater success through greater persistence.

There is no failure. Setbacks are integral to the way Universe-H works to provide ever more granular fodder for its expansion.

Conveyor-Belt-of-Life

Let's look at the Habit-Duo from a different perspective.

Whether obvious or not, for the tens-of-thousands of years (50 to 100-thousand) Homo sapiens have existed on this planet. Unquestionably, everything we now know and enjoy as technology and all that will become 'reality' in the future has always been here: just a perception away.

Stated differently, as our cognitive capacity is about the same as for our first ancestors. We do not so much neuro-physiologically process differently but instead, as a consequence of understanding the granularity of vastly more impacting-events, form quite different attitudes and perceptions.

Stated differently, we are not so much evolving but instead, by flooding our neural storehouses or data-archives with thousands of times more fodder or action-potential, expanding our inherent ranges processing capabilities to accommodate the increase.

Thus, as long as the curiosity pro-habit is given free reign, one is significantly more inclined in our current decade to recognize patterns already provisioned by Universe-H. Therefore, in reality, we do not invent but instead uncover what is already Out-There.

In other words, although one directly creates neither the Out-There nor the specific Deluge from which fodder springs, it is however possible to exert some control on Bombardment-Sphere 'impact-event' possibilities. For instance, one can decide to get out of the hot tropical Sun and into the shade.

Regardless, all are gifted with a phenomenal resource, Devise-Mulling, which can independently spirit degrees of awareness and conscious intervention.

Devise-Mulling is incredible because its continual activity ferrets out and utilizes populated data-archives to remix possibilities (myriads of frequency variant action-potentials) and create E-Puzzles that inspire Solutioning and therefore 'discovery' or more exactingly **uncovery**.

Look around you. To a lesser or greater degree, others have not only diverse behaviours (notably mostly comprised of habitual responses) but also differing values and 'stuff'.

Significant for **Way Better** Your L.I.F.E^2. discussions is that the majority of peoples behavioural habitual variability was developed in their formative years: i.e., not by choice but due to domestication carried forward by others domesticated before them, and before them, and so on.

Regardless, we tend to get wiser as we age due to the process that has been functioning the same way since birth (perhaps even before): i.e., one's particular Bombardment-Sphere provisions a broad range of sensory-impact events that vary in both frequency and intensity.

Crucially, those events that 'land' on or are sufficient to stimulate active or **ready-state** frequency-appropriate neurons get sensory-accepted and converted into action-potential **fodder**.

Thus, fodder is what builds one's data-archives and determines habitual actions. In other words, because recognized current-new results in immediate patterned-responses, habitual-response is actually 'what we became used to' during domestication.

Fortunately, as one continues to experience new Bombardment-Sphere impact events, one's neural processors become more proficient at comparing **current-new** to **archived-old**.

More proficient simply means that as a data-archive continues to be populated, Devise-Mulling and/or Cognition-Complex can more accurately 'predict' from more highly populated (higher action-potential) data-storehouses, the likelihood of potential outcomes and thus make recommendations via issuance of **Test-It**s to either avoid or approach the incident.

In this way, therefore, all exposure initiates within ones environment or Bombardment-Sphere. It literally provides 100% of the cognitive **fodder** that creates Tier-five (and other) data-storehouses.

> Pertinently then, it is the action-potential content within data-archives that dictate the quintessence of one's perspectives, behaviours, Cognitive-Habits or Experience-Senses and all other aspects of who one is and is becoming.

Conclusively then, exposure dictates experiences, which ultimately manipulate one's perspectives, attitudes, behaviours and thinking.

Therefore, one's Bombardment-Sphere, which is feeding one's sensors is better oriented to provide uplifting rather than damaging events.

Perhaps obvious is that if you have not been exposed to something, it will be **UN-**recognized by both Body-Self and Mind-Self.

In the best of all conditions where limiting or chaos-habit Experience-Senses, were not so prevalent (i.e., having strong GO-TO action-potentials) all new information would be storehoused with applicable intensity.

> Bias and self-doubt chaos-habits can manifest as belief there are such things as kings and queens and/or religious 'leaders' which know better how to better run your life.

Point is that when established biasing chaos-habits are in charge new information, which would allow new thinking will be intensity downgraded or bypassed by Cognition-Complex in favour of the tried-and-true GO-TO Cognitive-Habits that sustain ones Experience-Sense of 'normality'.

It was thus for our ancestors for about 50 millennia. Tribal members, under the dictates of tribal leaders were kept busy focussing on survival basics for most of the day.

As each 'subject' totally bought into their specific societal role or fabricated function, the possibilities all around them were simply downgraded by their Cognitive-Habits and thus not perceived.

> If this seems similar to why your day runs the way it does, it should: so usurp your chaos-habit dictators by creating new pro-habits.

Even today, dictates of others, both direct and indirect drive one's living-experiences from non-supportive family to degrading employers.

There just may be a 'rat-race' escape module however. Begin by creating a pro-habit that sustains the fact no-one is superior and you have the right to know. Such is the driver in first world countries that enable easy access to quality education and the internet.

The internet tool is amazing because it can provide enormous quantities of excellent fodder and thus build huge data-storehouses, which Devise-Mulling, if set free from bias Cognitive-Habits can maximize to create Puzzles to answer complex questions. No wonder, with so many variant perspectives, so much 'stuff' is available today.

Apparent and contrary to thinking of even 15 years ago, data-archives can sustain massively huge quantities of action-potentials, whose limits, excitingly have not yet been even closely reached.

> When unfettered, I term the vast array of possibilities the **Conveyor-Belt-of-Life**.

Although foddering can easily become overwhelming, it is incredible to realize that most people actually have vast genetically provisioned data-storehouse reserves.

To summarize then, others not only have different thoughts or more accurately thought sequences but also because of their particular interaction with their distinct Bombardment-Sphere have unique perceptions and Experience-Senses.

As one's cognitive mechanisms compare current-new to archived-old and as deficient data-archives will 'blind' you to possibilities, so it is with the Conveyor-Belt-of-Life: you can't take from it, what you can't perceive or more accurately that which Experience-Senses do not allow you to have familiarity.

Look around. You can see others have the relationships and things of which you dream. However, for some reason, even though you are definitely as worthy, they do not seem attainable or possible for you.

This attitude exists because your Cognitive chaos -habits are disallowing positive action by downgrading event intensities and thus excitement by interjecting chaos-habits such as fear, self-doubt and Chatterbox.

Without excitement, Devise-Mulling Puzzle creation, which is responsible for all expansive thinking is limited. Resultantly, chaos-habits foster and validate false perceptions, feelings or Experience-Senses that your desires are not possible for you. Critically as well, without Devise-Mulling involvement you can never give it your all.

How does one overcome restrictive Cognitive-Habits, which manifest in their chaos-habit form as biases, self-doubt, depression, addictions, etc.?

Only one way is available.

Whether excited by what you are doing or not, get more excited!

In other words, you can take control of both your Cognition-Complex and Devise-Mulling facilities by consciously getting excited.

It is absolutely possible to create an excitement pro-habit. Get excited about whatever you are **DO**ing, otherwise your outcome will continue to be ho-hum.

This is so because both intensity and data-archive population extensiveness are the determiners of whether chaos-habits or pro-habits will be the **GO-TO** ones.

This is easy to substantiate. Right now, think of something you previously did that really excited you.

Now recall as many details as you can in the next 30 seconds or so. Of course, not only were many details available for recall but also the recall process was effortless and stress-free.

Now try to remember the fork you picked-up to eat dinner last night. Recollection is probably impossible because it was simply not exciting enough to deliver any significant action-potential: that is unless you accidentally jabbed the tines into the palm of your hand.

Therefore, here is the answer to getting what you **TRULY** want whenever you **TRULY** want it.

Get excited; get involved; expose yourself to huge numbers of different **UN**-recognized and/or higher-intensity situations and **DO** everything with passion.

You are not only 'worth' as much and have the same rights as the person next to you, but also can have as much fulfillment and 'stuff' as him/her: providing you **TRULY** believe you are worthy and it is possible for you!

Therefore, continually change your Bombardment-Sphere as this will resultantly alter your sensory-acceptance. Cyclically **DO** this changing until all your purposefully created pro-habits get you what you want from the Conveyor-Belt-of-Life.

Second Key: In that about 98% of the world's problems have to do with money, there are lots of people out there stirring the 'pot' in many unpredictable ways. Therefore, a little diversity is recommended. In other words, five small incomes will not only provide diversity but produce the same return as one bigger revenue stream with far less stress.

A great pro-habit to develop is **spending-avoidance**. To countermand its chaos-habit nemesis **spending-impulse** one should understand the difference between needs and wants.

Needs are survival in the moment: whereas wants are discretionary. Sure, you would like to have it: but is it survival dependant. If no, then put the purchase off until you have built vast surplus: then re-evaluate its usefulness and your desire. Chances are the new model will be better anyway.

Following are some of the most overlooked money-wasters. Convenience stores seem nice but all their items are priced using the impulse-buy not the bargain-price retail-pricing model.

Cell-phone plans are notorious for getting you on fixed contract and then offering a better deal to new customers a few months later: check your plan often and negotiate hard. They do not want to lose your business so will be flexible.

The same process is applicable for T.V. and internet plans. Not only look for cheaper but also do not pay for blocks of channels you seldom watch.

Don't order pop or water beverages at restaurants. This is especially true of fast-food establishments as their markups are hundreds of percentage points. Wait for sales at grocery stores or buy wholesale at your discount store and take some along. Ask for regular water when at a sit-down restaurant and save.

Movie houses are notorious for massive overcharge. If you calculate the price you are paying for each kernel in a bag of their popcorn, its staggering. The popcorn is typically over $100.00 per pound.

Bank fees can be extreme especially at ATM's. Eliminate all seldom or unused bank accounts that charge a monthly fee: this can be huge.

Don't buy magazines at a newsstand or at any store checkout. If you like the publication, an annual subscription on promo can be less than two magazines cost at the newsstand.

Billions are needlessly spent on interest that can be avoided. Pay all credit card balances when due. If not, at least pay minimum to stop compounding charges. Also little known is that you can call and get your rate reduced.

If you need money, it is better to get a loan from a bank: this can save thousands per year.

Try some of the following to add small amounts to your monthly revenue because many small incomes can not only exceed one big income but also spread the risk. Save 10% of earnings through automatic disbursement and invest in government bonds; invest in dividend yielding stocks from blue chip companies; save coins; write a book or pamphlet on some specialty; get people to donate the things they don't want and sell them in garage sales; rent out a spare room; host students; the list is endless. Find what you like to do and monetize it.

Economists suggest putting a percentage away each month. This works if you can stay dedicated to it.

A simpler alternate method really works as well. I used this method starting the day my son was born, and still use it 30 years later.

Each time I make a purchase, I only use 'paper' money not coins. In other words, instead of spending change to fulfill the residual amount of the purchase, I break a new bill then put that change in a jar at the end of the day.

For example, when I purchase a coffee and muffin that costs $ 2.30, I will use a $ 5.00 bill. The $ 2.70 change will be saved. If I purchase another coffee and muffin, I would again break a $ 5.00 bill resulting in another $ 2.70 change: even though I could have used my available change for the second purchase.

Some days I have over $ 20.00, which all goes into coin jars. My intention was to save this for my son so that he would have a fund from which he could withdraw 20% for discretionary purposes and save the rest for his education.

The first time he and I counted the money when he was five, his 20% was substantial. This successfully taught him the power of saving and gave him many thousands of dollars toward his education. Today, Brandon is one of the rare Lawyers with a Summa Com Laude business degree.

Point is this method is painless and it works: Nothing like having surplus cash to reduce one of the daily stresses of debt and financial scarcity.

When you go to a grocery store and buy a chocolate bar, the cash you have acquired for the purchase probably seems inconsequential to you.

For other items however, it is just a matter of degree: whether you put the unencumbered cash down for a lamp, a fridge, a car, a plane or getaway mansion on some favorite island, belief in self-worth is the common factor that enables or disables one from picking what they **TRULY** want from the **Conveyor-Belt-of-Life**.

Wrap-up

Universe-H has been around a lot longer than have we Homo sapiens. In fact, if the 13.8 billon years our universe has existed was allocated on a 365 day calendar, January 1st being the Big-Bang beginning, then hominids (our direct ancestors) arrived on the scene on December 29th (about 3 million years ago) and Homo sapiens on December 31st between 23:56 and 23:58   (100 to 50 thousand years ago, respectively).

Spectacularly, somewhere between 2 to 4 minutes Universe-H time, Humans have gone from orphans existing on a spinning ball of iron and rock in a massive universe without any concept of its true properties to uncovering enough of its basic rules to get off the planet and into space.

Leaps

How is it possible that in such a very short time, the human species has managed to accomplish such leaps? Especially considering that so many other species either became extinct, like dinosaurs (and countless others), which dominated for hundreds of millions of years or life forms like bacteria, which have existed for billions of years have not evolved to do what we can do?

The *Way Better* Your L.I.F.E[2]. series is all about exposing humanities differences in regards to **How-We-Truly-Work** and how we fit into Universe-H: A monumental task to say the least.

The journey of uncovering How-We-Truly-Work has been a fascinating quest because illuminating the parameters of How-We-Truly-Work has required also explaining how our Universe-H works as well.

In other words, how Universe-H has provided all the stable ingredients to make life, living and exponential Figure-It-Out Puzzle Solutioning, which substantially explains how we have accomplished so much, possible.

Since its Big-Bang inception, Universe-H's energy components and 'mass' spin-offs have been in dynamic motion. These two manifestations account for everything we can currently 'observe' (and extrapolate) in Universe-H.

Manifestations range from infinitesimally small energy building blocks through to the many variant and overwhelmingly large 'mass' accumulations of nine-hundred million mile plus diameter stars with core temperatures greater than 5 million degrees.

Stars are incredible life instigators. Before exploding and distributing their elementary products throughout Universe-H, Star furnaces cooked and pressured Hydrogen into the essential elements of life over billions of years.

Critically, if during all this massive activity, vibration of Universe-H's fundamental energy building blocks were unstable in any way, not only would Universe-H be a substantially different place with everything mushed together but also life as we know it would not exist.

Thus, it is because Universe-H's **Base-one** energy components are absolutely frequency constant that all its products from elementary particles (protons, neutrons and electrons) through elements, compounds and onwards into more complexity also are stable within their operating ranges.

> Notably, even the elements that are 'unstable' according to physics criteria are not random, because they predictably decay at constant rates.

In other words, if the essential drivers of our physical-selves, i.e., iron, calcium, sodium or potassium to name a few did not present constantly but instead randomly morphed to become something else with different properties, we and all other Eukaryote life (as well as Archaea and Bacteria life forms) could not and would not exist.

Thus, absolutely Key is the stability or SAMENESS of the foundational Universe-H energy building blocks of mass, which support the propagation of life. Indeed every observable aspect of Universe-H (and probably those yet 'unobserved') is critical for our existence: at least as we understand existence to date.

Way Better Your L.I.F.E^2. emphases understanding our mechanism functionalities for a specific purpose: so we can better utilize their workings and interactions to get what we TRULY want. That said and understood: the obvious place to initiate explanations to encompass all the **How-We-Truly-Work** processes was determined to be the **Out-There** itself because that is where external Bombardment originates.

Tracking Bombardment from the millisecond it 'strikes' our biology is useful for true understanding because it allows discussions to flow from sensory-array apparatus, which are designed to initiate uncovering what is going on **Out-There** through to how physiological mechanisms work to spirit not only movement or actions but also one's behaviours and personality.

Additionally and excitingly, one came to understand the inseparable relationship between not only how integrally Universe-H and we Homo sapiens function but also one's place and purpose within our Universe-H Home.

Fundamentally, we are genetically predisposed to store sensory-accepted information for one broad-scope purpose: survival.

However, survivals front line warriors (Soma-Habits) can only work effectively when a sensory-event is recognized.

Significantly, recognition is a gradient (as is everything else in Universe-H) from unfamiliar (unpopulated data-archives) to slightly familiar (minimally populated data-archives) to expert (significantly populated data-archives).

So … what are the implications of recognition-status for not only **How-We-Truly-Work** but also the offered strategies to *Way Better* Your L.I.F.E^2.?

Actually, three fundamental aspects are critical to understand regarding **How-We-Truly-Work** because they enable more-useful outcomes.

First, original or first time **Out-There** contact is always **UN**-recognized and of higher intensity.

Second, one's primary survival strategy for Body-Self sensory-accepted events first takes the form of rapid and **event-relevant** Body-Self responses or Soma-Actions first and Cognitive-responses second.

Third, action-response effectiveness (for both Body-Self and Mind-Self) is a direct correlation to the action-potential population of frequency-matched data-archives.

In other words, survival is much more likely when a sensory-event is recognized than when **UN**-recognized. Obvious upon reflection is that responses in new situations are mostly less than useful. For instance, think how unwieldy was the first time you tried to print the letters of the alphabet, use a spoon or drive.

The reason for imprecise responses is Comparative-Analysis dependence on interlacing of current-new with frequency-matched archived-old.

Remember from previous discussions that interlacing is necessary so that Body-Self and/or Mind-Self mechanisms can match and therefore select the correct frequency-matched Patterned-responses, which of course have been built from repetitive previous exposures to frequency-similar sensory-events. Thus, our species has great reliance on experience as the 'teacher'.

Without the process of utilizing current-new to select appropriate response-patterns, which remember engage appropriate Body-Self (patterned) movements, one could, instead of brushing an annoying fly off your bare arm with one's hand, might instead slap their cheek.

Thus, when (current-new engaged) data-archives storehouse sufficient action-potential, appropriate and timely patterned-responses are instigated to correctly adjust ones position within one's Bombardment-Sphere. Alternately, when affected data-archives are minimally populated fledgling response-patterns can result in wildly inaccurate and potentially dangerous actions or inactions such as 'freezing' to the spot.

In other words, when archived-old is minimally populated, outbound patterned-responses, which action as Soma-Habits and/or Cognitive-Habits will also, due to lack of repetitive similar experiences, be ineffectively formed and therefore imprecise.

Training to enable rapid Body-Self response (Soma-Habit creation) is well understood to increase performance. Performance of course is the catchword utilized to describe desired, response-pattern automated (i.e., without Cognitive-Alerts and therefore Mind-Self intervention) precise actions.

One relies on Soma-Habits throughout most of one's 'normal' or uneventful day.

Soma-Actions are great because when sensory-events are both recognized and lower-intensity, they deploy automatically and quickly. Quickly is Key to survival and made possible because Body-Self mechanisms operate about 1000 times faster than Mind-Self's. Rapid response capability is due to both less sophisticated neural real-estate and limited processing options.

Adaptively, Body-Self's quick adoption of the Soma-Habit 'flight' response to extract one from danger is a genetic baseline utilized when Body-Self data-archive population is lacking or minimal in regards to **UN**-recognized and/or higher-intensity current-new.

It is Mind-Self however, which upon both analysis of the Body-Self tailored Cognitive-Alert (in **UN**-recognized and/or higher intensity situations) and incorporation of Visual-Array sensory-data (through Cross-Sensory-Bundling) that assesses whether fight (a Cognitive-Habit) might better serve.

The upshot is although genetics has provisioned data-archive functionality and capacity (massive for Mind-Self), sensory-array contact with the Out-There is what both populates data-archives and consequently provides the basis for extended comparative-analysis of Mind-Self's current-new to archived old.

> Key is that only conditions that inspire awareness are **UN**-recognized and/or higher-intensity.

Thus, human genetic upgrades, which provide massive storage capacities and processing capabilities, gifts us with special functionalities that for Body-Self are rapid-responses and for Mind-Self more considered-responses.

Thus, Body-Self can be relied upon for survival, while its Self-Duo Mind-Self collaborator not only provides survival enhancement but also living-condition improvement.

Living-condition improvement is accomplished through powerful **Figure-It-Out** processing mechanisms that enable choice via its Comparative-Analysis arsenals, which permit **significantly-similar** not just Body-Self's SAME archived-old.

Universe-H provides steadfast: we provide expansive.

Expansive design is phenomenal. It is one's segue into creating one's own Pro-habits, which when effectively made the **GO-TO**'s (and deposing destructive chaos-habit counterparts) will automatically (as this is the nature of habits) get you what you **TRULY** want.

> Don't misunderstand the importance of **TRULY** though: PASSION is the ABSOLUTE key to ensuring highly populated data-archives and thus massive and pertinent recall.

In other words, TRULY means that you are so passionate about whatever is being sought that nothing will get in the way of your attainment.

> Novelty thus trumps almost every chaos-habit.

In other words, when involvement is **TRULY** passionate, Figure-It-Out will engage CP3 and CP4's awesome Cognition-Complex and Devise-Mulling arsenals.

> Recall, only by engagement of these mechanisms is awareness, higher consciousness and therefore true sentience possible.

Spirited together, Cognition-Complex and Devise-Mulling will create broad-scope Puzzles, which when Solutioned by the extensive flow of current-new (inspired by passion) will massively populate appropriate Tier-one through Tier-five data-archives.

Thus, cognitive Pro-habits will become the GO-TO's and thus, second-by-second get you what you TRULY want. It is an utterly fantastic design!

Of course, passion breeds passion. At least this is realizable when you create new pro-habits where you both allow yourself excitement for extended periods and disengage those domesticated chaos-habits that told you to sit still and be passive.

Dream on my friends: Passion-dream on!

Addiction Disengagement

Know two absolutes: first, that addictions, compulsions, negative self-talk, damaging behaviour, overeating and the like are automated detrimental **chaos-habits**; and second that you can choose to create new Pro-habits to **Pro**-ductively benefit you while simultaneously usurping those nasty chaos-habit harbingers.

Chaos-habit GO-TO Habit-Power presents within a gradient or range from minor to dominant, as do all aspects of Universe-H.

'Minor' and 'dominant' are of course evaluations of living-condition impact. In *Way Better* Your **L.I.F.E^2.** jargon these two terms are intended to underline the degree that a chaos-habit like addiction impacts one's living-experience possibilities: from slightly to massively detrimental.

> Detrimental means to what extent an addiction chaos-habit keeps you from not only being all you can be but also feeling or experiencing all the wonders being provided from **Out-There**.

As stated earlier in **Tactics**, Cognitive-Habits do not stand-alone but intertwine in a complex weave where if you 'pull' on one, others will variably stir into action as well.

Regardless, the concept of Pro-habits and chaos-habits is powerful because one can readily determine whether an action or contemplated action is going to be more-useful or less-useful in regards to getting what one TRULY wants.

Remember, both Soma-Habits (Body-Self) and Cognitive-Habits (Mind-Self) are genetically provided survival tools. Cognitive-Habits or Experience-Senses however additionally embrace living-condition acceptability or what one finds satisfactory and 'normal' - comfort-zone if you wish.

Habits are awesome because they keep doing what they do and keep us safe with little cognitive attention, maintenance or awareness of their Habit-Power.

Key though is that Habits are a direct consequence of sensory-acceptance, which in turn is a consequence of one's Bombardment-Sphere conditions.

> In other words, although genetics provides the capacity, living-conditions (one's second-by-second Bombardment-Sphere environment) dictate, via sensory-acceptance, one's data-archive content. Let me explain by a short example below.

Speaking and listening are both Cognitive-Habits that have been honed from years of repetitive exposure to others in one's environment. Thus, 'language' or the data-archiving of noises (words) or frequencies yields speech modalities, which are similar in accent, tone and speed to others in one's circles-of-influence.

> For instance, those of you who have friends who grew up speaking another 'language', like French for instance, although their new vocabulary may be excellent, tonality no doubt contains remnants of the their original language. Such is the tenacity of Habit-Power.

Think of Habit-Power in terms of your own domestication. If you were continuously exposed to substance abuse like drugs and alcohol, abuse or overeating throughout your young years, chances are these sensory-accepted events became the Psychological or Cognitive-Habit 'norm'. You just accepted them.

Therefore, in later years as similar current-new events arise, no alarms go off. This is because current-new is recognized by comparative-analysis processors, which therefore summarily deny any living-condition revaluation.

> It is Cognitive-Habits then, through repetition, which also exert their heavy-hand to keep us flowing down the middle of one's **habit-flume**. It is useful to picture one's habit-flume as a simple water flume where water is channeled down and in the middle by gravity, not up on the sides.

To create improved living-conditions then, perspective changes in regards to your view of your self-doubt chaos-habit through positive Pro-habit creation is critical. Otherwise, fear and anxiety chaos-habit **L.I.F.E^2.** stoppers will cause unnecessary anguish.

Habit-Power will absolutely manifest
What you believe you **TRULY** deserve
Whether beneficial or detrimental to your **living-experiences**.

Kudos if you are in an addiction-intervention program - whether for pharmaceutical substance abuse, overeating, anger or whatever, you are already taking powerful steps to create new and more beneficial Pro-habits.
If you TRULY desire to *Way Better* Your **L.I.F.E².**, Key to double underline is that SAME is not useful!

Good news is, from a neuro-physiological perspective – i.e., the actual structure of your brains neurons, there is nothing to stop you from Pro-habit creation. However, from a Habit tenacity perspective, your two worst chaos-habits, self-doubt and Chatterbox will vigorously impede.

> Previous discussions underlined that Chatterbox is a domesticated habit: been around a long time.

Both of these chaos-habits have become the GO-TO's through decades of action-potential reinforcement. Thus, on presentation of higher-intensity current-new corresponding Tier-5 Experience-Senses or Cognitive-Habits can be triggered.

For instance, if you are addicted to smoking, watching someone else smoking (current-new remarkable-event) will no doubt initiate Cognitive-response patterns, which will habitually-dictate your similar reactive behaviour.

Voila, your addiction manifests. It even 'feels' right because Cognitive-Habit design provides an Experience-Sense of comfort and safety as long as you are proceeding down the center of the habit-flume: i.e., well within a Cognitive-Habits gradient-of-acceptability.

Bad news is you are never going to get rid of old chaos-habits.

Way Better news is that you don't have to.

You get to do an easy loping end-run, which means just ignore chaos-habits, and begin the creation of any Pro-habits that will support your quest toward what you TRULY want. You have to TRULY want it though as previous discussions have underlined.

You just cannot fool your brain into action via the 'pretend' chaos-habit because it is your brain, no one else's.

Take control of you back by utilizing the simple and always effective way.

Get passionate about what you want and keep striving toward it.

Endeavour until the new Pro-habit data-archives are sufficiently populated and the new Pro-habit becomes the GO-TO: i.e., is chosen instead of its detrimental chaos-habit nemesis.

Do not worry about what your chaos-habits tell you are setbacks. Chaos-habit resistance is just trying to keep you in place or down the habit-flumes center.

Powerfully, chaos-habits manifesting tells you are on the right path to Pro-habit creation.

Note that inbound current-new frequencies spirit recall: no choice in that unless you dramatically change your Bombardment-Sphere like going to a movie, running or listening to music, skydiving, etc.

We love to be entertained because unfamiliar current-new substantially reduces or even mostly eliminates familiar frequency cuing. Thus, one has no data-archive 'triggering' comparatives to recall.

In other words, as we now know, fledgling data-archives free us from comparative analysis of current-new to archived-old, which in turn frees us from both assumptive thinking and dredging up negative Experience-Senses or debilitating chaos Cognitive-Habits like self-doubt and Chatterbox.

Freed from chaos-habits even for a minute feels really good. This is because Movie-of-You-Life processors are free to present your 'reality' with mostly current-new content that has not been filtered, mollified and dampened by negative chaos-habit interceptors.

Conclusively then, we are designed to compare current-new to archived-old. This is awesome when supportive Pro-habits are being incorporated but not comforting when chaos-habits are marauding and skewing one's perspectives toward the negative.

'Recall' is a phenomenal process that mobilizes data-archive action-potential by duplicating it into **action-drivers**. Action-drivers are great because they can mobilize more and more recall.

Cascade-recall is useful when retrieving the granularity of an interesting adventure but not-useful when unpleasant recall content is being negatively spun by chaos-habits.

However, with a little practice the initial **recall-surge** need not trigger debilitating cascading-recall.

With a little practice and determination one can create an intervention Pro-habit that disengages further recall.

The purpose of the 'Intervention' Pro-habit is to interrupt ongoing (current-new triggered) archived-old recall by inserting a **time-space** between the initial recall-surge and Cognitive-Complex's reactive Puzzle creation.

All are aware trials-and-tribulations happen while living. Importantly, the **control-scope** you give to both your Chatterbox and self-doubt chaos-habit sets will determine which reactive Experience-Senses will be deployed.

Experience-Sense selections of course, depending on their Habit-Power gradient from innocuous to debilitating will skew perceptions because current-new is either being 'spun' negatively by Cognition-Complex or in the most damaging scenario curtailed due to processor overload.

When negatively skewed both perceptions and competencies about one's capability to deal with unfavorable events will be correspondingly unfavorable. Additionally debilitating is that one will feel overwhelmed and helpless.

Chatterbox is of course trying to reinforce your unworthiness by telling you that you should have done better – what an idiot – you're just not capable: you know all that demeaning negative stuff, which is its wheelhouse.

Tell that miserable destructive Chatterbox, in the loudest meanest voice possible (yes out loud) to shut-up and go away. Tell it that it no longer has control of you by presenting false negative values. Tell it you now understand the 'Past' does not exist except as I give permission for my Chatterbox to negatively sway the recalled events, which are bogus anyway.

Tell Chatterbox that you just will not take its bullshit anymore. Tell it you are going to create a **Support-bot** Pro-habit instead that is kind and friendly; that will assist in honing more useful choices until Support-bot Solutions how to get what I **TRULY** want.

When young, how many times did the following occur. You were told no, that's not right; you were pushed aside so someone else could do it 'right'; or you were bypassed because you were (in your perspective at the time) being viewed by others as not capable?

How many times did you imagine having the power to reject those who rejected you?

Be it older siblings, parents, aunts, uncles, schoolyard bullies or whomever these occurrences all reinforced your sense of unworthiness. In other words, you gradually began to give up trying and just Public-Self accepted your place in the pecking order while your Private-Self became less-and-less your fan.

You should be your biggest fan! Never let external-locus events tell you whether your acceptable or capable: you are. Remember chaos-habit mandates are to keep everyone in place.

Habits are not you: you are just allowing them control.

One's sensory-acceptance is determined by their Bombardment-Sphere or physical environment of the moment.

All Habits have the same modality: perform the same way over-and-over. Such steadfastness is great because only by their consistent nature can they rapidly respond us to safety.

Nicely you can take control back by creating your own user-designed Pro-habits that you can trust to work on your behalf.

Simultaneously, you can also usurp chaos-habits that are detrimental to your fulfillment. A foundational starting-point is with the most predominant Cognitive-Habit: The Way-You-Think.

The superior Pro-habit tack is to perceive setbacks (those things that do not turn out as you wanted) as fodder (truly data-archive fodder) that was storehoused so that next attempts will be closer to the mark.

> In other words, do not allow or give false-gauge chaos-habits permission to curtail your attempts. Instead, develop the tenacity Pro-habit by time-spacing Chatterboxes attempts to keep you SAME through negatively presenting you to YOU.

In *Way Better* Your **L.I.F.E**^{2}**.** terms all data-archives populating is a good thing. In no way is acquired experience a failure. Consider that the true measuring stick is how much experience was gathered not just the outcome.

In other words, a more useful 'appreciate' Pro-habit perspective is to understand that all fodder-acquisition provides Comparative-Analysis with more frequency precise selections so the next reiterations will be more useful.

> Fodder storehousing and recall are Keys to How-We-Truly-Work.

When you keep striving, for sure you stand a far superior chance of becoming all you can be. Most critically, this is so because possibilities are endless when you keep **DO**ing.

> Thus, **DO**ing is Key to both How-We-Truly-Work and getting what you **TRULY** want.

Abuse-Cycle

> Before you consider yourself to be incompetent, unworthy or a loser

> First, ensure that those to whom you are comparing yourself
> are not just power hungry bullies using your air to fill their emptiness.

Let me ask you a question. Are the abuses happening to you right now? If not, let me also ask you what do you think makes them seem real? I suggest it is because you are letting your low self-esteem chaos-habit turn you into the abuser as well as the abused.

I get that your situation was horrific and that you then felt unworthy, betrayed, helpless, etc.

Both the Past and the Future are not real.

Don't nurture and drag your past into your present
because for sure you will mess-up both your present and your future.

However, it was definitely the abusive person that had poor values not you: it was and is not your fault in any way. Do not let them vicariously control you by allowing Chatterbox to mix archived-old memories in with current-new sensory-events and create Puzzles that through endless rumination cause you stress and turmoil.

If abuse has ended and you are giving permission to reacting to the recall as if it is real, you have transitioned into being both the abused and the abuser.

Control is the automated nature of both Soma-habits and Cognitive-habits. Soma-habit control is all about rapid and immediate response to Body-Self sensory-accepted millisecond-by-millisecond events. Soma-habits genetic mandate is to get away from dangerous events on a macro level: such as, pulling your hand away from a flame.

Cognitive-habits, although they may seem fast are no match for Soma-habits: in fact they are hundreds of times slower when instigated by Body-Self Cognitive-Alerts. Cognitive-habits are slower because Soma-Self has already begun positional Bombardment-Sphere adjustments prior to delivery of the Cognitive-Alert to Mind-Self.

Additionally and I think amazingly, Mind-Self has a daunting, reiterating task list that must remain pertinent to the flurry of Cognitive-Alerts caused by the occurrence of a significant current-new event sequence.

Following are a few of Mind-Self's interactive and Cognitive-Pathway overlapping responsibilities. Initially Mind-Self must decode the Cognitive-Alert: as to not only the Body-Self location(s) being disrupted but also the intensity of the event-string. Evaluation of fluctuating intensity is critical as the 'choice' of Cognitive-Pathway also determines how much of the finite neural-processing capacity is used.

Mind-Self must bring Visual-Sensors on-line by issuing Test-Its to Body-Self that appropriately home-in on the affected Body-Self parts as well as logging in any other remarkable-features, which may also be a threat.

Mind-Self must utilize Cross-Sensory-Bundling to decipher which visual events are pertinent to received Cognitive-Alerts, then pro-actively scope-out and cascade-evaluate one's now rapidly changing Bombardment-Sphere (as Body-Self is in motion) that have potential to cause additional disruption (i.e., remarkable-features).

Concurrently, Cognition-Complex, depending on intensity will be variously engaged in tailoring assorted complexities of Test-Its, which it designs to yield granular Body-Self adjustments not only to optimize positions for safety but also to provide better visual-sensory feedback: like quickly looking around a corner to assess threat.
All of this type of control is great because it dramatically enhances survival potential. Problem is tenacity is only an incredibly great feature, if it is a Pro-habit being deployed but not so much when a chaos-habit is driving you to destruction of one kind or the other.

However, when Bombardment-Sphere conditions are not survival threatening and cognitive chaos-habits negatively drive your seconds, minutes and hours by twisting perceptions through bogus mixing of archived-old with current-new, their control is not a good thing.

Pro-habits can be created that will absolutely uncouple the chaos-habit grip.

Only once one recognizes the harmful impact of chaos-habits can one begin creating Pro-habits. Start by PASSIONATELY saying in a very loud voice, "I'm done with negative chaos-habit control". You might add on "I am creating, beginning right now, user-friendly Pro-habits that benefit me instead"!

Say this aloud multiple times a day: make it a mantra. In this way, you will begin to build those Pro-habit data-archives until your chosen new Pro-habits, beginning with the Pro-habit of knowing you can take control back, become the GO-TO's.

Engagement with the world substantially morphs into a deep sense of joy when you create Pro-habits that accept and allow love and belonging for yourself and others.

May not have much control of recall but you can create a filtering or selective pro-habit set that gives you full-control over your interaction with it. You can actually put a **time-space** between any current-new event and your reaction (or no reaction) to it.

In other words, control of initial-recall is unlikely because it has been frequency-cued upon a Bombardment-events sensory-acceptance. However, one does have full control of what is done with the recall.

Create an interference pro-habit that enables the insertion of a time-space between the initial event recall and any cascading-recall. In this way, by choosing to disengage additional recall, one can absolutely neutralize debilitating recall-based reactions such as addictions and self-abuse.

Pro-habit creation Considerations

This section summarizes Key factors that are necessary to not only create Pro-habits that will automatically serve you but also usurp all sorts of domesticated chaos-habits that keep denying you what you truly want.

To create any new Pro-habit the fundamental, top of the list **Key** is **TRULY** or passion. Passion is necessary because the more excited you are the more you will **DO**; and the more you **DO** the faster are populated the required data-archives; and the faster the data-archive population, the faster will the new desired Pro-habit become the **GO-TO**.

> In addition, as we have learned, the more often the new **GO-TO** Pro-habit is utilized, the quicker the nemesis chaos-habit neural-real-estate will be used for other purposes; therefore degrading chaos-habit power even further.

You truly cannot fool your brain, or Devise-Mulling in *Way Better* Your **L.I.F.E**^{2}. vernacular, by pretending to be passionate and committed. Also be aware that for many, denial of excitement is high on the domesticated list of chaos-habits that substantially interfere with creating new Pro-habits: remember the "sit still and behave scenario".

If your current surroundings do not inspire your passion or are defeating passion by triggering Chatterbox and undesirable self-doubts, then change your Bombardment-

Sphere or external mosaic, so that archived-old is not triggered by familiar current-new.

> In other words, enroll in groups with common desires and goals, as this will always provide unfamiliar current-new, so you can get on with the gusto of creating Pro-habits. Excitement breeds excitement, so support groups are great whether for addictions, health or writing books.

The 'DO'

'**DO** and keep **DO**ing' is an intertwined close second Key to rapidly creating robust Pro-habits: total immersion with passion is the goal. Remember the task-at-hand is to super populate new Pro-habit data-archives while starving chaos-habit data-archives.

> Nothing happens without THE "**DO**"!
> The more "**DO**", the more **L.I.F.E²**.

There is a principle I call the '80/20 rule'. What it means is that as one strives for whatever they TRULY want, only about 20% of ones sensory-acceptance and therefore experiences will be directly useable to accomplish the final goal.

The other 80%, even though not directly applicable is absolutely necessary to enable Comparative-Analysis to explicitly select pertinent archived-old from a copious population of significantly-similar. In this way, experience breeds experts that have enormous granular knowledge.

Our species is phenomenally gifted. One reason is due to our amazing Devise-Mulling facility whose dual purpose is to both formulate and Solution Puzzles (E-Puzzles).

> Devise-Mulling is the arena that creates and invents, and thereby fulfills Mind-Self's extended 'survival' mandate: to improve living-conditions.

Additionally amazing is that Puzzle formulation, through remixing well-populated data-archives into almost unlimited combinations and permutations is possible from either aware choice or unaware mulling (as in dreams or surprising 'ideas').

As detailed in "Mind-Self", Solutioning or Figuring-It-Out and finding The-Ways is accomplished by Devise-Mulling cascade-tailoring Test-IT's that inspire specific Body-Self actions and consequently provide ongoing specific to Test-IT sensory feedback-loops.

Point is, do not worry when your striving (Devise-Mulling) does not seem to be hitting (or even close to) your preconceived mark, as you only need 20% to be massively successful!

> The other 80%? … well … it is essential experience that will absolutely guide you away from future mistakes and toward ever higher aspirations.

As far as Chatterbox goes, you will just have to keep telling it shut the heck up until it finally does. Chatterbox is one resilient chaos-habit that will tenaciously try to derail you at every turn.

However, now you can call it by name and interrupt its GO-TO power by creating an interference Pro-habit you can begin to relegate it to the junk heap where it belongs. Do not let up though, because it is not your friend or fan. Each time it pipes up with its negative nastiness, tell it (scream at it if you can) to shut up and go away.

Generally, it is beneficial big time to name your chaos-habits because this helps you understand not only their characteristics but also what conditions trigger them.

> In other words, once you know them by name you can take them out of the game and put them on the bench where they might make a fuss but at least not on your playing field.

A great way to disengage chaos-habits is to laugh at the absurdity of their Habit-Power over you. Remain diligent and do not let 'beat-up' chaos-habits tell you that you are failing: as long as you are striving, you are absolutely NOT failing … tell them in a very loud voice to GO-AWAY.

Movie-of-Your-Life

Finally, let's review the actual mechanics of the processes, which present one's 'reality'.

Remember **Self-Duo**'s task is about uncovering 'What is going on **Out-There**' and then spiriting physical movements within ones **Bombardment-Sphere** that optimize safety or minimize termination risk. To accomplish this enormous feat, **Body-Self** and **Mind-Self** deploy multiple neural processors that Comparatively-Analyze **current-new** against frequency-applicable **archived-old**.

In other words, by integrating current-new with frequency appropriate archived old, appropriate Body-Self and Mind-Self action sequences are engaged purposed to maximize survival potential.

Throughout learning How-We-Truly-Work, one fact surfaced as irrefutable: mechanism processing is not instantaneous.

In other words, handling the tumultuous flow from sensory-acceptance through action-potential morphing, fodder storehousing, recall, Comparative-Analysis, Puzzle creation, Solutioning, Test-It formulation, Self-Duo actions etc. takes time.

The demands on both Body-Self and Mind-self mechanisms are never-ending. Hugely complicating is that mechanisms, while effectively managing limited neural-resources must operate 24/7 without warning as to event-occurrence, event-intensity (from dulcet to tumultuous) or event-duration. The inbound flow is anything but constant and reliable.

We do not so much aimlessly bump around through our physical environment as do Bacteria but navigate around within our thus ever-changing Bombardment-Spheres.

Navigation is enabled by an incredible and specialized neurological facility that presents one's 'reality' as an ongoing movie, which I call the **Movie-of-Your-Life**, whose responsibility it is to represent its version of 'What is going on **Out-There**'.

Stated differently, the integration and virtual animation of all aspects of the copious quantities of variant data-flow from both Cognitive-Alerts and Visual-Sensors is the responsibility of the **Movie-of-Your-Life** presentation center.

It is continually hard at work ensuring holistic continuity of one's reality experience. Fortuitously and incredibly, the Movie-of-Your-Life production is mandated to virtually present one's reality without interruption, sputtering's, pauses or blank spots.

In this amazing Movie-of-Your-Life facility, 'remarkable-features' from both Cognitive-Alerts and Visual-Sensors are superimposed over background CP-5 and CP-4 Soma-Sensor and Cognitive-Sensor data-flows to present one a virtual mosaic of continuous and situationally appropriate, yet integrated event-progression over a synchronous flowing backdrop.

Shocking as this may be, 'Sight' is an illusion. One does not actually 'see' Bombardment-events in real time but instead a Cognitively processed rendering that is not occurring in the eyes at all but being presented in Movie-of-Your-Life neural real-estate.

Therefore, like dreams that provide 'visual-images' by dredging and morphing archived-old, visual-processors render copious current-new (billions of bits of visual-sensor information per second) into the mix that the Movie-of-Your-Life presents as current reality.

As Visual-Sensors are cognitive senses, Mind-Self utilizes cognitive processors to create a cohesive 'sight' rendering of what is going on Out-There. Things only 'look' the way they look to you because visual-processors use Habitual preponderance to rapidly present their interpreted illustration product as mental image that we call sight.

Diagrams

IS-101: **Self-Duo**

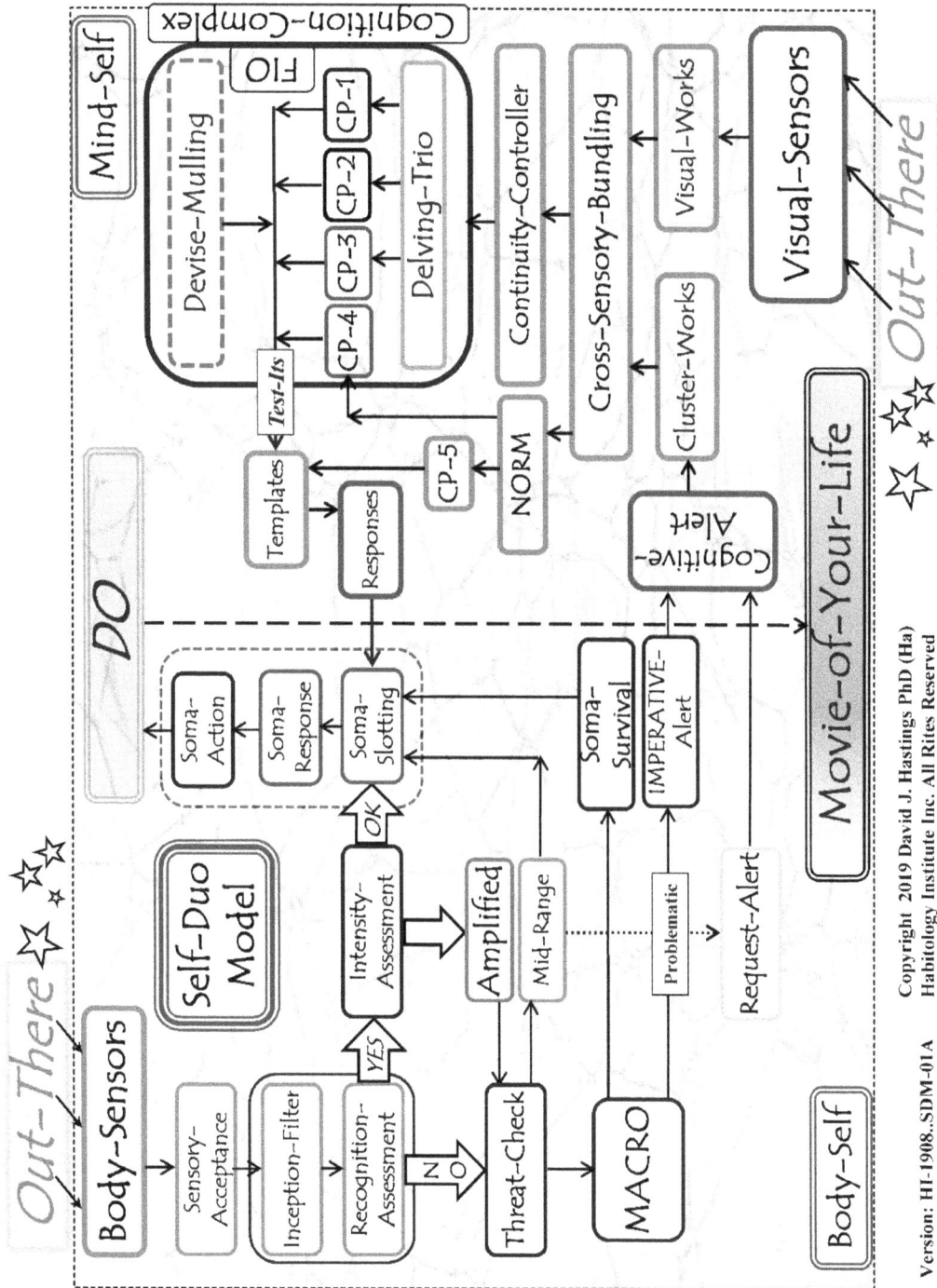

IS-102:

Version: HI-1908..SDM-01A

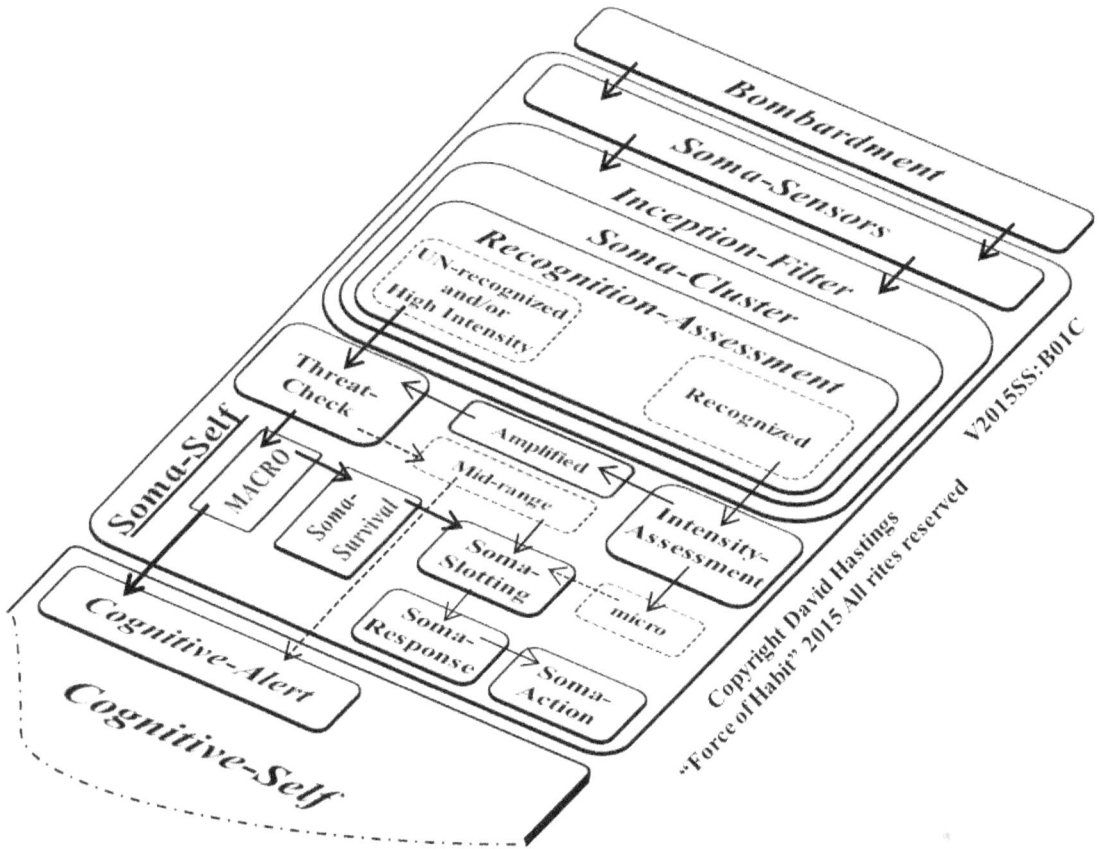

IS-103: **Cognitive-Pathways Model**

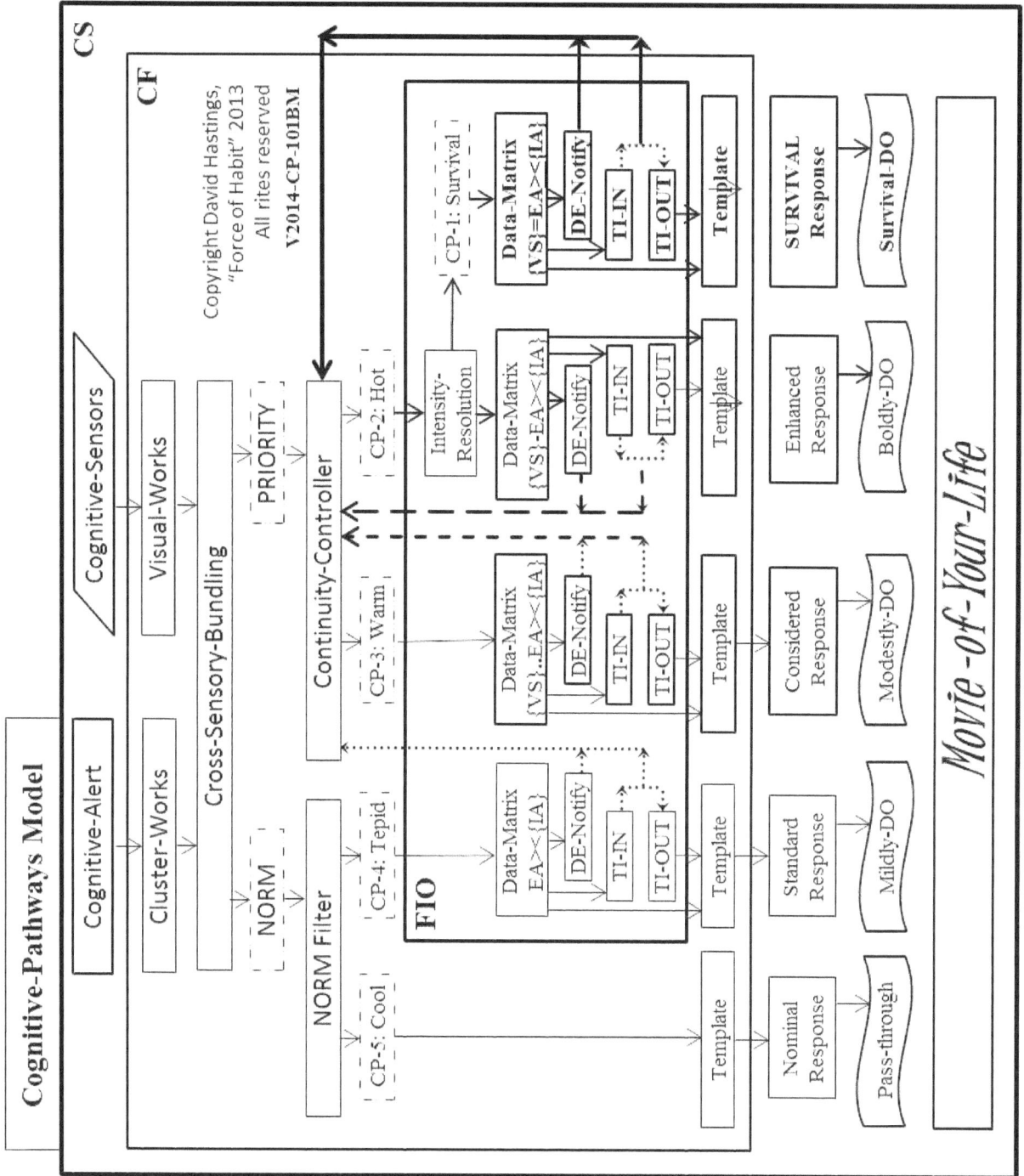

Cognitive-Pathways Model

CS

CF

Cognitive-Sensors

Cognitive-Alert

Cluster-Works

Visual-Works

Cross-Sensory-Bundling

NORM

PRIORITY

NORM Filter

Continuity-Controller

CP-5: Cool

CP-4: Tepid

CP-3: Warm

CP-2: Hot

CP-1: Survival

FIO

Intensity-Resolution

Data-Matrix EA><{IA}

Data-Matrix {VS}:EA><{IA}

Data-Matrix {VS}:EA><{IA}

Data-Matrix {VS}:EA><{IA}

Data-Matrix {VS}=EA><{IA}

DE-Notify

DE-Notify

DE-Notify

DE-Notify

TI-IN

TI-OUT

TI-IN

TI-OUT

TI-IN

TI-OUT

TI-IN

TI-OUT

Template

Template

Template

Template

Template

Nominal Response

Standard Response

Considered Response

Enhanced Response

SURVIVAL Response

Pass-through

Mildly-DO

Modestly-DO

Boldly-DO

Survival-DO

Movie-of-Your-Life

IS-104: The Ways: Solutioning

Originating with **Data-Matrix** this model expands the **Figure-It-Out** module to disclose many granular data-handling processing events.

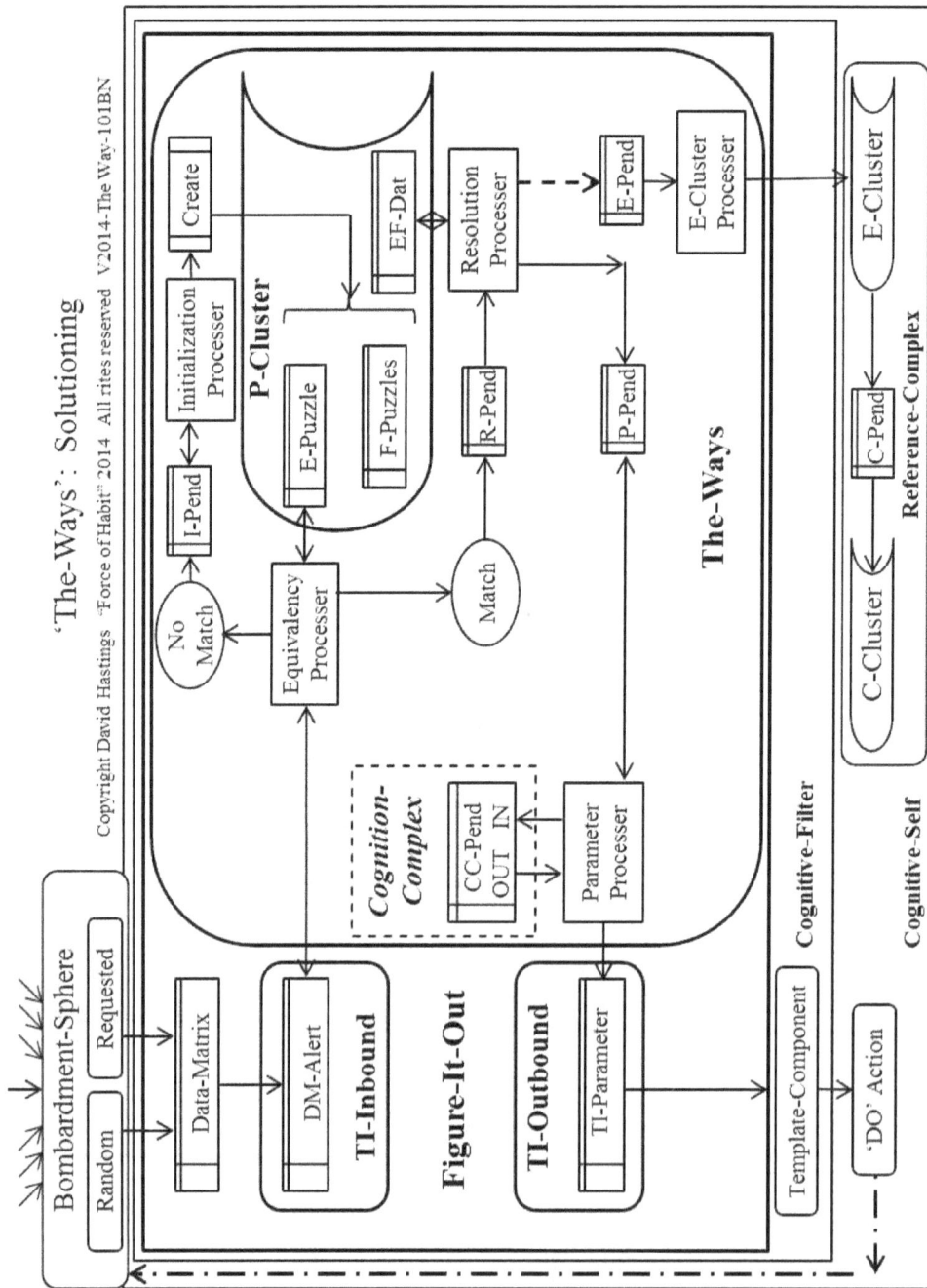

IS-105: The Ways: Proactive

Spirited by both **Resolution-Processor** and **Initialization-Processor** populating **P-Pend**, this model expands Figure-It-Out **Parameter-Processor** and Cognition-Complex's **Delving-Trio** processing functions. Additionally, it introduces **Devise-Mulling**, which is one's self-directed volition link to interact with the **Out-There**.

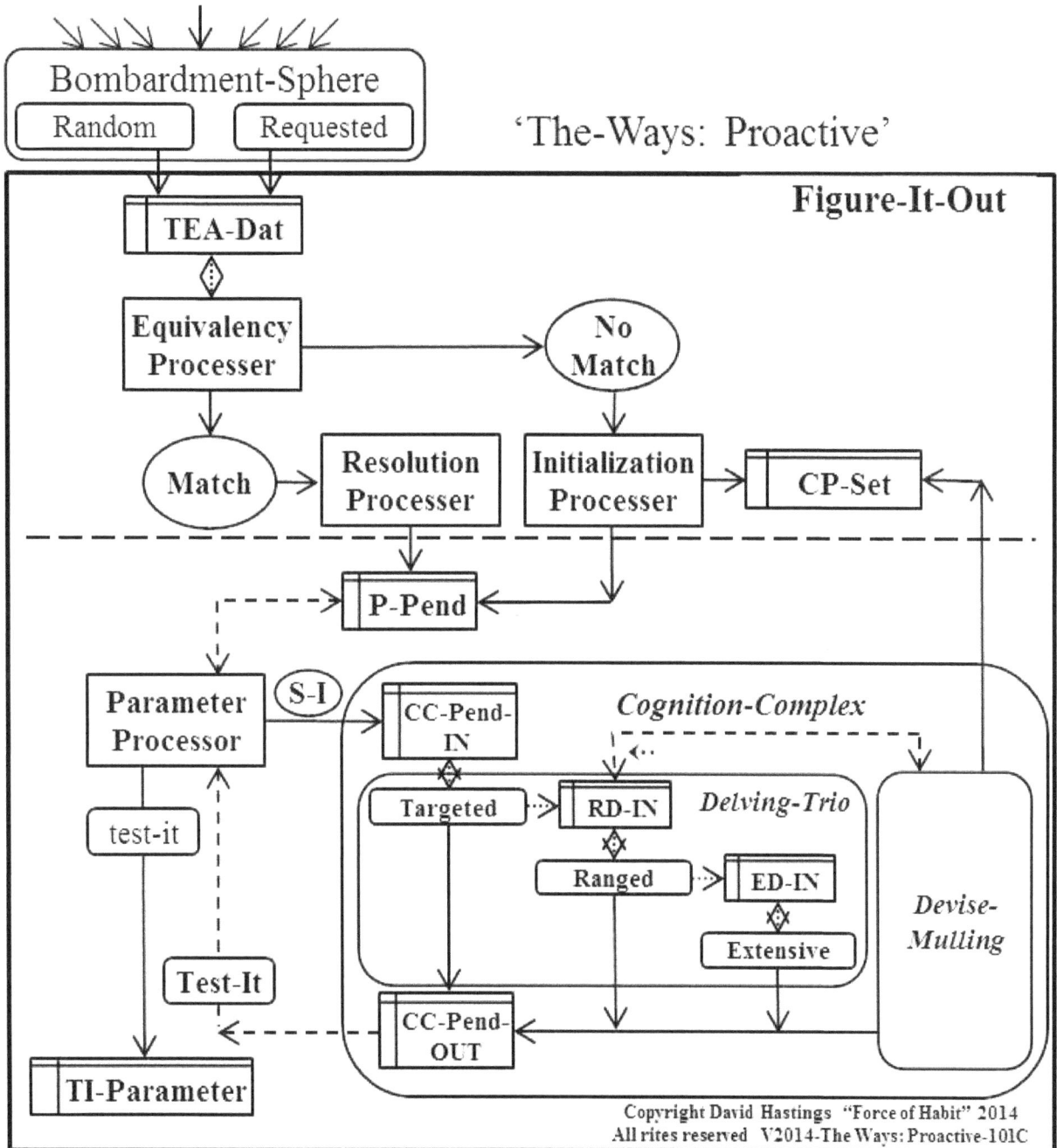

Bombardment-Sphere
Random
Requested

'The-Ways: Proactive'

Figure-It-Out

TEA-Dat

Equivalency Processer

No Match

Match

Resolution Processer

Initialization Processer

CP-Set

P-Pend

Parameter Processor

S-I

CC-Pend-IN

Cognition-Complex

Targeted

RD-IN

Delving-Trio

Ranged

ED-IN

Extensive

Devise-Mulling

test-it

Test-It

CC-Pend-OUT

TI-Parameter

www.ingramcontent.com/pod-product-compliance
Lightning Source LLC
Chambersburg PA
CBHW080459110426
42742CB00017B/2946

9781775066101